Bible Readings

FOR
TEACHERS

ABOUT THE AUTHOR

Ruth Stenerson writes this book out of many years' experience as teacher and author. After teaching high school for seven years, she attained a master's degree in English from the University of North Dakota, Grand Forks. She presently serves as associate professor of English at Bemidji State University (BSU) in Bemidji, Minnesota. Her articles have appeared in various Christian journals and devotional books. Her work has also been published in the *Minnesota English Journal.* She wrote and compiled a *Handbook for the Bible as Literature* which is used as the text for a course she teaches at BSU.

Bible Readings for Teachers is Stenerson's second volume in this devotional series, following her latest book, *Bible Readings for Singles.*

Bible Readings

FOR TEACHERS

·

Ruth Stenerson

AUGSBURG Publishing House · Minneapolis

To my students—
especially those who over the years
have become cherished friends—
and
to my colleagues who
have over the years shared with me
in the family of faith

PREFACE

All honest work is honorable; those who do it are to be respected. Those types of work in which the end is service to others have a special kind of satisfaction, and those who do such service rightly find joy in the doing. Teachers who by education and personality are suited to and dedicated to their work know that joy, even when their task is not an easy one. It often is not easy in our day, for many reasons. Teachers are leaving the profession in large numbers, yet many remain in it with satisfaction for a lifetime.

At its best, the relationship between a teacher and a student is a very personal one, dependent on what each as a person is. If the relationship is right, the outcome can be rich and productive. We all know President Garfield's words to Williams College alumni when Mark Hopkins was their president, "Give me a log hut, with only a simple bench, Mark Hopkins on one end and I on the other, and you may have all the buildings, apparatus, and libraries without him." We had better keep the libraries and the rest, but we know what he means. And we have felt the challenge to be like Mark Hopkins.

Those of us who are Christian teachers have a greater challenge to face than Mark Hopkins. We know the Great Teacher who, in a minor province of the Roman Empire, taught fishermen and tax collectors and women, and the world was never the same again. He teaches for us the methods class par excellence.

Those of us who are Christian teachers know a source of strength and renewal that comes to us through our daily devotional life and through the fellowship of believing colleagues. I am deeply grateful for the abundance of that fellowship I have known. I pray that through these devotions that bring you to the written Word and to the living Word you may be empowered and given the grace for each day's needs, the joy of young people to love and to serve, and the endurance that overcomes the tensions of constant preparation, of tedious paperwork, of demanding discipline, and that endless need to cope with the "daily-ness" of our lives.

The most important part of each page is the selection from the Bible itself. Please read it before you read the meditation. The prayer on each page is only a beginning. Between the last word and the Amen your own prayer will continue your conversation with God. Be sure not to forget the listening part. God bless your reading!

■ AN OLD PROFESSION

2 Chron. 17:1-11: "They took the book of the Law of the Lord and went through all the towns of Judah, teaching it to the people" (v. 9).

Teaching is as old as the human race. Already in the Garden of Eden God taught man that acts carry consequences. Later some of his star pupils— Abraham, Isaac, Jacob—were given a great deal of personal attention. Careful instructions were given to Hebrew parents about their responsibility as teachers of the young. When, periodically, reformers among God's people attempted to bring them back to a right relationship with him, they turned to teaching from "the book of the Law of the Lord."

Some complain in our day that teaching is no longer respected as it once was, that parents look upon teachers as baby-sitters, that beginning engineers are paid as much as their professors who have taught a dozen years.

Perhaps it is true that teachers are taken for granted in our day and that our salaries suggest that we would have done better in another vocation. But it is still true that teaching is a noble and needed profession. Just as the elders of Judah taught the people (adult education already!), so we today can know that the work we do is needed, respected by thoughtful people, and a blessing to our society. We have no need to apologize for our role.

 Great Teacher, we are honored to labor in a vocation in which we share your activity. Grant that we may honor you. Amen.

Share today with another teacher who looks discouraged your conviction that you share a job full of worth and dignity.

■ TRUSTING YOUR JACOB

Gen. 35:1-15:   "God said to him, 'Your name is Jacob, but from now on it will be Israel' " (v. 10).

Jacob, in his early years and even well into manhood, is hardly the person one would think a likely choice for God's purposes. He conspires with his mother to defraud his twin brother of the birthright. He cheats Laban by building his own flocks at Laban's expense (though Laban had treated Jacob badly too), and he deceives Laban by leaving the country without telling him or letting him bid farewell to his daughters. He is a deceitful operator. One would expect God to say, "I have wasted my blessings and visions upon this man. There is no honesty in him." But he does not. He has chosen Jacob, and he shapes him until Jacob takes his place with Abraham and Isaac as one of the great patriarchs of his people.

We as teachers sometimes find Jacob among our students and even among our colleagues. It would be easy to decide, "There is just no honesty in that student. I can't trust a thing he says," or "I know better than to trust what that colleague says about me." Yet as God keeps working with Jacob until he becomes Israel, so we too are called never to give up on other people. We cannot know what God may have in store for them.

Lord, I am grateful that you have never given up on me. Grant that I may never give up on anyone I work with. Amen.

Find some way today to open an opportunity for a student who has not performed in a trustworthy way to change his reputation.

■ TRUSTING EACH OTHER

Exod. 4:1-17: "You can speak to him and tell him what to say. I will help both of you to speak, and I will tell you both what to do" (v. 15).

Most of us have heard someone else report what we have said and have wanted to cry out, "No! That's not right! You forgot to include . . . I didn't say it that way. . . . You changed my emphasis. . . . You misinterpreted me." We probably do not have too much trouble believing that God is telling *us* what to say, but it is harder to accept the reality of his being behind what we would rather not hear our colleagues saying.

There is no indication in the biblical story that Moses found it hard to accept God's telling Aaron what to say—at least until Aaron's fiasco at Mount Sinai. Both of them, in their dealings with Pharaoh and with their own people, held clearly to what God had told them to speak. If they had not cooperated in those crucial hours, the whole exodus experience could have been jeopardized. To what a marvelous degree God leaves the success of his plans to human voices!

Also to what degree the education of students is left in the hands of those of us whose jealousies, headaches, or antagonisms can reduce our effectiveness! We need to trust that God can tell our colleagues what to say as well as ourselves, and that he will teach us too.

 Lord, help me not to act as though I have a monopoly on the wisdom and love you impart. Amen.

Watch for an opportunity today to be supportive of a colleague.

■ UNBROKEN COMMANDMENTS

Exod. 20:1-21: "Moses replied, 'Don't be afraid; God has only come to test you and make you keep on obeying him, so that you will not sin' " (v. 20).

To "break" a commandment or to "break" a law probably was originally a metaphor suggesting a tablet of clay on which a law was inscribed and which had been deliberately broken to pieces. But as it is used in our language, the phrase is not accurate; it gives a false impression. When a law is disobeyed, it is not the law that is broken, it is the integrity and reputation of the one who disobeys the law that is broken. Given the continued practice of disobedience, the character of the person is what crumbles. The law remains intact, in force. Especially the law of God stands firm, built into the moral order of things.

Our students live in a time and a society in which disobedience to the law is not only countenanced but often considered smart. Many learn within their own homes that what is wrong is not to *do* what is immoral or illegal, but to *be caught* at it. Income tax cheating—provided one can get by. Speeding—if one isn't caught. Lying—if it makes a situation more comfortable. By example and word, we need to reinforce their sense of right and wrong. Truly, "God has only come to test you and make you keep on obeying him, so that you will not sin."

Lord, give me the kind of moral integrity to be a right example for my students. Amen.

Stop to think about what area of moral concern poses the greatest temptation to your integrity, and to that of your students.

■ INDIVIDUAL INTEGRITY

Exod. 23:1-13: "Do not follow the majority when they do wrong" (v. 2).

The criticism is sometimes made of our schools that their purpose is not to educate individuals but to train children to be cogs in the same wheels in which their parents have been cogs. Teachers, so the critics say, avoid leading students to ask the profound questions that, in spite of their difficulties, need to be grappled with.

For example, by what right do we as Americans continue to use such an exorbitant percentage of the world's nonrenewable resources? If that is selfish and wrong, how do we get off the merry-go-round that says that is the way to live? How do we avoid, in our teaching, reinforcing those values that can be maintained only at the cost of the deprivation of others? Is it any excuse that most of us are engaged in reinforcing those values—teachers or not? Sometimes it is hard to hear the music when we ride on the bandwagon.

Students and teacher alike will find it difficult to make individual decisions on gravely serious issues. But God commands, "Do not follow the majority when they do wrong." To obey him, we will need to be real individuals, able to make moral choices we can live with and defend.

Lord, show me how to be an individual of integrity in a society that calls me to follow the crowd. Help me make that integrity appealing to my students. Amen.

Find a constructive way to be different from the crowd, a way your students can respect and admire.

15

■ THE PERFECT MATCH

Exod. 35:20—36:6: "Everyone who wanted to, both men and women, brought . . . all kinds of gold jewelry and dedicated them to the Lord" (35:22).

Four times in this account we find reference to "those who wanted to" or "were able." Not all the people were to share in the building and decorating of the tabernacle in the wilderness: only those "who wanted to." These were to be assisted by two men to whom the Lord had given "the ability to teach their crafts to others." What an effective combination—those who were willing to learn with those to whom God had given the ability to teach! Paul, much later, refers to one of the gifts with which the Spirit equips the church—those "to whom God gives the ability to teach others." Our lives are to be God's methods classes whereby he makes us effective teachers of those who are willing.

No matter how potentially effective we may be, to teach those who are not willing remains a dubious, if necessary, effort. We cannot, like Moses, exclude those who are not willing. Moses had such a response to his plea that finally people had to be restrained from bringing more. We face a real challenge not only to be open to God's gift of the ability to teach others but to stimulate the unwilling to become the willing. For that too we need the Spirit's enabling.

 Lord, I pray that you will develop in me ever more fully the ability both to teach and to stimulate the unwilling to become willing. Amen.

Try to find a quiet moment to talk to an unwilling student about his dreams for the future and the way his education can help.

■ THE HOLY AND THE COMMON

Lev. 10:8-11: "You must distinguish between the holy and the profane, between the unclean and the clean" (v. 10 NIV).

In our text, Moses and Aaron as priests are assigned the duty of teaching their people. Their teaching was to go beyond facts to the far more subjective matter of distinguishing between "the holy and the profane, . . . the unclean and the clean."

Not everyone in our society agrees that the teaching of values is the proper activity of the schools. Some say that should be left to the home, the church or the synagogue, or such support groups as Boy Scouts or Camp Fire Girls. Others believe that schools have a necessary role in helping students develop values important to society.

Can teachers really become involved with their students without being teachers of values? The values we have as individuals are such integral parts of our characters we can hardly keep our students from knowing what they are. Our reverence for the holy, if we are Christians, will be evident in our attitudes toward the sacredness of life itself. Our language and the stories we tell reveal our choices between clean and unclean. For our students to get to know us as people without knowing something of our values is almost an impossibility. The responsibility laid on Moses and Aaron is ours too.

 Dear Lord, may my influence be such that my students are helped in developing positive and life-enhancing values. Amen.

Make a list for yourself of five values important in your life. Emphasize one each day of the coming week as it fits your activities.

■ RESPECTING GOD'S EARTH

Lev. 25:1-22: "But the seventh year is to be a year of complete rest for the land, a year dedicated to the Lord" (v. 4).

How important for us as teachers by word and example to teach respect for the earth on which we live! Almost daily, newspapers contain word of the results of man's lack of respect for the earth. Acid rain, nuclear waste, depleted water resources—these and many more are problems that stare at us.

To teach a youth to be a respecter of the earth rather than a polluter is often to encourage him to go against attitudes in his home. In spite of the seriousness of many environmental problems, many of us Americans still operate by the principle "If I can afford it, I can have it." President Harding has often been criticized for his shortsighted satisfaction with "peace in our time," but we continue to pollute air and water and use nonrenewable resources as if nothing matters so long as they last for our time.

Often a way to reach an unconcerned parent is through a concerned child. In a cartoon, a college-student daughter at the dinner table says, "How can I be motivated to care about the starving if you keep passing me the chocolate sauce?" Maybe our own attitudes are the ones we can do most about. From our own respect for the earth and resources God gave us, our students can learn both the facts and attitudes that will help.

 Dear God, help us to use our environment wisely and to teach others to do so as well. Amen.

Find an effective poster on the need for respect for environment and use it for a classroom bulletin board.

■ REMEMBERING THE PAST

Deut. 4:1-14: "Be on your guard! Make certain
that you do not forget, as long as you live, what
you have seen with your own eyes. Tell your
children and your grandchildren . . . " (v. 9).

I have never been really sure that Henry Ford
actually said "History is bunk," but if he did he
surely was in disagreement with Moses. Moses
placed the responsibility squarely on the Hebrew
parents to teach their children their history—
especially as "his-story," the acts of God among his
covenant people. "Tell your children," Moses commands over and over. A people who know where
they have been in their past have a better opportunity
to know where they are going in their future.

No matter what we teach, we have a responsibility
to help our students know and understand their
past so they may know their situation in the present
and their direction for the future. How tragic if we
should allow our students to forget the sad human
history of racial injustice (how soon it could
intensify!). How sad if we forget what Vietnam
should have taught us! How sad for Christianity
in our land if it should continue its apathy toward
world hunger and political corruption!

We too need to listen to Moses say "Be on your
guard. Make certain that you do not forget . . . what
you have seen." We need to teach the lessons of the
past to our students.

> Lord, keep me mindful of the lessons I have
> learned from experience that can be helpful
> to my students. Amen.

**Make a list of five lessons you have learned from
the past decade. How could they help your students?**

■ REPEAT THEM!

Deut. 6:1-12: "Teach them to your children.
Repeat them when you are at home and when you .
are away, when you are resting and when you
are working" (v. 7).

The ancient Hebrews taught the Torah to their
children in the same way the army teaches foreign
languages—total immersion. The laws which governed
an entire way of life for the child were taught at
every possible moment and in all kinds of life
contexts. No halfway measures were sufficient.

How often as teachers we are aware of the many
things we need to cover in a day or in a grading
period or in a year! Where can we find time to teach
with the thoroughness the task demands? No wonder
parents and administrators call for a return to basics
when we cannot cover everything a student needs
to know in this complicated world.

Part of our responsibility as teachers, within the
bounds permitted us, is to make choices among the
multitude of things it would be *nice* for a child
to know and those it is *essential* for him or her to
learn. Each of us must learn what is that humanity
we share with every other living person, what is our
right relationship to the earth which sustains us,
what is our source of life and our purpose in it.
Those things we need to know so well that no human
greed or lust or war can make us respond in a less
human way.

Lord, help me to make right judgments about
what is important. Amen.

**Set clearly in your mind today three of your personal
priorities in working with students and watch for
opportunities to emphasize them.**

■ THE OPEN HAND

Deut. 15:7-18:   "Give to him freely and unselfishly,
and the Lord will bless you in everything you do"
(v. 10).

In a society in which many are affluent and even
more have enough to meet all needs, if not all wants,
students who don't have money to spend as others
do can feel very inferior and may try to keep their
predicament a secret from almost everyone. I have
sometimes discovered, usually too late, that students
have disappeared from my classes because a text was
too expensive to buy and they were embarrassed to
reveal this problem. They evidently felt their lack of
money to be a sign of their lack of worth. It is hard
to be poorer than everyone around us.

There is a great awareness of the poor in the
Bible. Many today look upon poverty as a sign of
laziness and incompetence. Biblical writers did not.
The poor are to be kept in mind, to be provided for,
to be looked upon as a sacred responsibility. Prophets
thundered at those who flaunted their wealth and
oppressed the poor. Our text says, "I command you to be generous to them." Do we have
opportunities as teachers today to watch for and
relieve problems of poverty as they appear among
our students?

Lord, help me to know when someone needs
the kind of help I can give. Amen.

**Read the book of Amos in the Bible, noting the
Lord's concern with the oppressed and the poor.**

■ ONE DAY AT A TIME

2 Kings 25:27-30: "Each day, for as long as he lived, he was given a regular allowance for his needs" (v. 30).

Jehoiachin was the king of Judah who was taken captive by the Babylonian armies of King Nebuchadnezzar and imprisoned while puppet kings ruled in his place with Babylonian consent. Jehoiachin's lot was a lonely one until another ruler succeeded to the throne of Babylon and decided to release the forgotten king. Then Jehoiachin was treated like a member of the king's household, an honored guest at the royal table for each day for the rest of his life.

Each day!—one at a time, inexorably one after another. Life is such a daily thing. At times that "daily-ness" becomes difficult to contend with. We plod off to school on Monday morning and we proclaim TGIF on Friday. If only there were more variety in the way day follows day!

Like Jehoiachin, we too have been given a daily allowance for our needs, and a place at the table of God. "Your strength will equal your days" (Deut. 33:25 NIV). We do not need to wait for that daily reinforcement as an enclosure with our paychecks. It is provided for each day's need. "Praise the Lord, who carries our burdens day after day; he is the God who saves us" (Ps. 68:19).

Lord, thank you for your daily support and salvation. Thank you for your availability. Amen.

Stop to imagine how difficult life could be in its dailiness if we had seven rather than five days to go off to work. Praise God for weekends.

■ LIVING CONSEQUENCES

Job. 31:13-28:   "If I did not, how then could I face God? What could I say when God came to judge me?" (v. 14).

Job has a magnificent sense of the relationship between act and consequences. He talks movingly of the three-sided relationship between his behavior toward others, his personal relationship with God, and God's relationship with him. Job knows that if his attitudes and behavior toward others around him have been wrong, selfish, or deceitful, he must give account when he faces God. If a servant has been mistreated, if food has been withheld from the poor, if gold has been hoarded greedily, God must be reckoned with. Job's is no crude, primitive ethic. It is still applicable today.

Working with our students, we teachers need to know how far-reaching the effects of our words and actions can be. What we have done or said returns to bless us (or to curse us), to bring us to account years later. I have been amazed to find how a student has remembered some words I have spoken and forgotten years before. Those words and acts have lived and had their consequences, as Job was sure they would. We need to consider that when God makes inquiry about their origin, we shall be accountable for them.

 Lord, thank you that your mercy washes us from our guilt for wrong words and actions just as your kindness blesses us for right ones. Amen.

If you had been the writer of our text, what aspects of your life would you have "worried about" in place of those Job mentions?

■ CHRISTIAN HUMANISTS

Psalm 8: "What is man, that you think of him; mere man, that you care for him?" (v. 4).

Groups of parents today occasionally express their concern about children being taught humanism in the public schools. To many in intellectual circles humanism is a good word, and those who express opposition are seen as narrow-minded. The word is not always given its right meaning. Strictly, it refers to the belief that human beings are capable of finding their answers to the human situation in themselves, usually implying a rejection of the supernatural. Those who express a confident faith in humanity but believe that God is the basis for that attitude may call themselves Christian humanists. It is true for us who are Christians that we do not see man as able to handle his own affairs without God's power and redemption.

The psalmist expresses a confident faith in man and his place in the universe. "You have made him inferior only to yourself," he says to God. The important fact is that God has given mankind a place of great importance in his universe—next to himself. Human beings did not remain what God had made them, true, but God did not desert them. He is still thinking of them and caring for them. We too may say "Up with the human race," but our confidence is in the activity of God on our behalf.

Thank you, our Father, that the answer we can give to "What is man?" is that we are your beloved children. Amen.

Stop to think about: What definition of mankind was used by Karl Marx? Machiavelli? Freud? Does that definition matter?

■ FACING THE UNEXPECTED

Psalm 24: "The Lord will bless them and save them; God will declare them innocent" (v. 5).

After decades of regularly increasing enrollments with ever greater numbers of teaching positions, few of us ever considered what would happen if the rate of population growth slowed. This was America, wasn't it? And was not the American way one of constant growth? As tax dollars began to contract, experienced teachers found movement upward or sideways stymied as school boards found recent college graduates cheaper to hire than experienced teachers.

Teachers are certainly not unique in finding jobs closed down before them. That happens far more bluntly in most kinds of work. But what does a person do in the face of the loss of his or her job at a time when new ones are hard to find? There is no easy answer. The loss of a job can be a rough emotional jolt, involving not only our financial well-being but our self-confidence and our faith in the system under which we have worked. In such a situation it is a challenge to be willing to "Proclaim with me the Lord's greatness" and to call upon others to "let us praise his name together" (Psalm 34:3). If we look unto him, we will in the end be radiant as we discover his will for us.

 Lord, help those who face the loss of their jobs to come closer to you in that experience. Amen.

Open the opportunity today to give a fellow teacher worried about job advancement or security the chance to talk out his worries.

■ TEACH *AND* . . . .

Ps. 25:1-10:   "Teach me to live according to your truth, for you are my God, who saves me" (v. 5).

Often when the Bible talks about teaching, it couples it with another activity. For example, Luke begins his gospel as a record of what Jesus began to *do* and to teach. The disciples in the early church set out to teach and to *preach* (Acts 5:42). Paul in his first letter to Timothy advised his young friend to "*command* and teach," and again to "teach and *exhort*." In Deuteronomy God tells Moses to "*write* this song and teach it."

We know well how many other activities share our lives with our teaching. Some teach and are homemakers; others teach and are cabinetmakers. Some teach and spend weekends as youth ministers in churches. Some are teachers and practicing artists. Some teach and do volunteer work. Some of us are nearing retirement and finding it all we can do just to teach.

As Christian teachers, what we do besides teach has a relevance to our Christian witness. Some of that time belongs to God. With him we look forward to a time when "None of them will have to teach his fellow countryman to know the Lord, because all will know me, from the least to the greatest" (Jer. 31:34).

 Lord, help me to do my share in your kingdom in those hours that surround my teaching job. Amen.

Count up the number of hours you spend in God's Word and service per week. Does it add up to a tithe?

■ MEMORIES

Ps. 25:6-22: "Forgive the sins and errors of my youth. In your constant love and goodness, remember me, Lord!" (v. 7).

Sharing memories is often delightful. When teachers and former students get together, they frequently say "I remember when. . . ." What follows may be humorous or poignant or moving.

The author of our verse is concerned about what memories about him may be in the heart of God. Evidently he has some memories about himself he would rather forget. He prays that God's basis for remembering be the "constant love" that is God's own nature rather than the sinful nature of the poet. He yearns to hear God saying, "I am the God who forgives your sins, and I do this because of who I am. I will not hold your sins against you" (Isa. 43:25). The prayer meets the promise. Now the psalmist too may forget those sins.

How God-like are we in forgetting the "sins" of our students? Do we, when students' words or behavior antagonize or anger us, tuck those memories away ready to be trotted out again to be used as evidence against them? There is one kind of failing memory that is no cause for concern—the kind that forgets the offenses of others. It is all too easy to have the kind of mental memory bank that keeps statistics of evil ready at hand.

 Lord, give me the ability to forget the failings of others as well as to remember their good qualities. Amen.

Examine your memory to see if there is an entry of someone's wrongdoing that should be erased. Ask God to help you release that memory.

■ THOSE IMPOSSIBLE DAYS

Psalm 42: "May the Lord show his constant love during the day, so that I may have a song at night" (v. 8).

No teacher needs to be told about the reality of those dull, awkward, uninspiring days when nothing we try brings a response, when we know we are uninteresting but can't seem to do anything about it. We hear or read of teachers who use weird gimmicks to add zest to their classes. They are successful, but we know that if we tried those devices we would only make fools of ourselves. Our colleagues bounce with enthusiasm and get glowing responses; we expend the same amount of energy but fall flat on our faces.

Fortunately we know too that these days are not always with us. If there are days when "he has sent waves of sorrow over my soul," there are also times when "once again I will praise him, my savior and my God." Experience quickly teaches us how our own dispositions affect the mood and attitudes of our classes. If we are dull and listless, the class is likely to become so. If we approach a class with zest and animation, we are more likely to meet those attitudes in return. Our days go better if we remember that "the Lord [will] show his constant love during the day, so that I may have a song at night."

Lord, keep me even-tempered and stable, supported by my awareness of your steadfast love. Amen.

Do a bit of research on yourself today. Note how your own mood affects that of your classes.

■ THE CLEANSED HEART

Psalm 51: "Create a pure heart in me, O God, and put a new and loyal spirit in me" (v. 10).

We probably had not taught long before some student had reason to apologize to us for some lack of courtesy or disobedience. In like manner, we probably had not taught long before we knew we needed to apologize to some student, perhaps also for a lack of courtesy or some put-down we realized had been unjust. We are at best imperfect beings and need to know where to come to be forgiven both by God and other human beings.

Attributed to David after he had taken advantage of Bathsheba at the cost of her husband's life, the psalm of our text portrays him as so aware of his great sin against God that he could see only that aspect of his sin, even though it had also resulted in Uriah's death. "Evil from the time I was born," he prays to be clean, to have "a new and loyal spirit," a restored joy, and a willingness to serve God better in the future.

We too need daily that renewal that comes from a cleansed heart, a redirected focus in life, and the fresh experience of joy that comes when we have confessed our sins. Our students may not know the reason for the difference that brings about in us, but they will sense that something has happened.

 Lord, create in me too a clean heart. Give me the openness and peace of one who is daily forgiven. Amen.

How long since you memorized some Scripture? Take time to learn some of Psalm 51 "by heart."

■ KNOWLEDGE OR WISDOM?

Psalm 90: "Teach us how short our life is, so that we may become wise" (v. 12).

As Americans we place high value on education. Our aim, we say, is to make it available to each youth to the degree that he is able to profit from it. We offer it as a remedy to social and economic ills —even moral ones. We respond with alarm to the idea that any other country can do it better than we. We attract tens of thousands of foreign students to our universities.

Yet we do not need to look far for evidence that people may be highly educated, with impressive intelligence quotients, without having what is necessary for happiness and contentment. Graduate degrees may be evidence of many years of schooling without their holders having found a way to fill the aching void within. They have much knowledge without the wisdom our text speaks of. They are empty, bitter, cynical.

St. Augustine wrote, "The heart of man was made for God and cannot rest until it rests in God." Pascal spoke of the "God-shaped vacuum in the heart of man." No matter how high the level of education or how many other advantages education has brought, if that God-shaped vacuum has not been filled, a person may still be an empty, unhappy shell.

 God of truth and wisdom, may your Spirit make us aware of our need for you to fill the inner void in our hearts. Amen.

Pray a special prayer of gratitude that you have come to know that the health of the spirit is as important as the health of the body.

■ IN PRAISE OF PRAISE

Psalm 98: "Blow trumpets and horns, and shout for joy to the Lord, our king" (v. 6).

When I read in the Old Testament the words ascribed to God himself, I come away convinced that God yearns for and enjoys the praise of his people. His nature is such that this recognition of his power and majesty and goodness are pleasing to him. The psalmist and, for example, the author of Job respond with their great poetry of praise.

If God is pleased by the praises of his people, how natural that our students, in the process of coming to deal with who and what they are, respond to our praises. Praise is powerful motivation for those who win it.

Not only God and our students respond to praise. Our colleagues need it too—especially those who may have sunk into a pattern of one year, then another, always the same. Perceptive praise for what they do well can enliven that pattern.

There is a fourth recipient of praise we need to keep in mind—ourselves. We can sense when we have done something well. We can encourage ourselves by recognizing our own successes and find impetus to go on to more of them.

Lord, I believe that by your grace there are things I do really well. I celebrate you today, and also my students, my colleagues, and myself. Amen.

At least three times today find occasion to openly express praise.

■ JUBILATION DAYS!

Psalm 100: "Enter the Temple gates with thanksgiving; go into its courts with praise. Give thanks to him and praise him" (v. 4).

Some days being a teacher is the most exciting and fulfilling life one can imagine. You know the kind of day I am talking about: the students are unusually alert and perceptive. Your colleagues—well, it's too bad there isn't more time during the day to fellowship with such fine people! Your administrator goes out of his way to mention praise of your teaching which has come to his attention. Your introduction to your subject led the discussion just the way you wanted it to go, and those socratic questions by which you developed your main points couldn't have been more successful. The hours flew by, and as you walked to your car you caught yourself grinning from ear to ear.

One of my friends would call that kind of day a "praise-God day." Not all days are like that, but what joy when they do come! What perfect opportunity to make use of the Psalms! Dozens of them resound with praise as the poets bless God's name, bring him thanks, and rejoice in his goodness. Join in and make a duet to God's glory. If tomorrow doesn't turn out to be that kind of day, you will have the memory of how you and the psalmist celebrated the day before.

Lord of joy and love, you know how we need those special days when everything goes right. Thank you for including them. Amen.

Letter one or two of your favorite psalm verses expressing praise on a card you can post on your bathroom mirror.

■ HOW GREAT THOU ART!

Psalm 104:   "Lord, you have made so many things! How wisely you made them all" (v. 24).

Facts and skills may be taught directly, but appreciation and a sense of wonder are as much caught as taught. Analysis of the structure of a moccasin flower is useful. The gasp of delight at its beauty may be even more likely to enroll a person unfamiliar with flowers as a protector of that lovely blossom. Our students, looking—even if unconsciously—for things to give themselves to, respond to our enthusiasms, our reverent hush, our cries of delight as much as they do to our theorems or our formuli.

One can hear in the words of Psalm 104 the poet's delight in what God has made, his awe in the scope of God's works. One can sense the reverent hush in "Lord, you have made so many things! How wisely you made them all."

Some people—even some teachers—seem so oblivious to the grandeur, the complexity, the beauty, the delicacy of nature around them as it bears witness to its Creator. How much better that students sense in us a glad delight in what God has done and in his provision for us!

 Lord, the beauty of the earth sings your praises. Give me a glad sensitivity to the wonders of your creation. Amen.

Even if it requires going off on a tangent—and usually it doesn't—find something awesome in the world around your classroom to share with your students.

■ YOU HAD BETTER MEAN IT!

Psalm 139:   "Examine me, O God, and know my mind; test me, and discover my thoughts" (v. 23).

I have always suspected that the poet's prayers for God's searchlight to be turned on him resulted from a feeling of uneasiness caused by his having simply *assumed* the right to hate with "total hatred." Awed by the sense of God's omnipresence, he may well have been nudged by God's Spirit into an uncomfortable wondering if he was entitled to the right to hate those he saw as God's enemies. History has shown some interesting cases of misjudgment on the part of those who assumed the right to decide the identity of God's enemies.

The prayer of our text is a dangerous prayer— it is likely to be answered. It is one we should all pray daily. The human heart is deceitful above all things and capable of rationalizing some strange attitudes as acceptable. As teachers we tend to see ourselves as unprejudiced, open-minded. Yet it is disquieting to be made aware of the amount of prejudice and stereotyping that hides in our hearts, sometimes leading us to believe it is our business to see another person as God's enemy and therefore one we can hate. God can protect himself. It is not our business to hate anyone. The command to us as Christians is to love.

Lord, shine your searchlight into my heart and make me willing to deal with the results. Amen.

Examine your own thoughts to see if you are trying to justify a hatred for anyone. Get rid of it!

■ OPENING THE DOOR

Prov. 2:1-15: "It is the Lord who gives wisdom; from him come knowledge and understanding" (v. 6).

Halvard, the aging contractor in Ibsen's *The Master Builder,* confides to a young admirer, "I've begun to be so afraid—so terribly afraid of the younger generation. . . . One of these days the younger generation will thunder at my door—they'll break through and overwhelm me." Wisely she replies, "I think that you yourself should go out and open the door to the younger generation. . . . Let them come in to you—in friendship" (Act 1).

Older teachers may easily be tempted to feel like Halvard when young teachers with fresh enthusiasm and newer ideas make their presence felt. Resentment and foot-dragging may readily grow out of the insecurity of older teachers who are suspicious of new methods and confident in their own, or who have observed older teachers eased out in order that younger ones lower on the pay scale may be hired.

All ages of teachers need to be understanding of others. Young teachers have much to contribute; their enthusiasm can be a real asset. The experience and life-wisdom of older teachers is a fund on which all can draw. As Titus reminds his readers, we are to "be ready to do good in every way . . . to be peaceful and friendly and always to show a gentle attitude toward everyone" (3:1-2).

Lord, help me to see and respond to what is good in people of all generations. Amen.

Watch your colleagues today to see what one thing you can learn from someone whose age is quite different from your own.

■ SETTING OUR STANDARDS

Prov. 3:21-35: "The Lord will keep you safe. He will not let you fall into a trap" (v. 26).

For a Christian to defend the status quo in contemporary society is becoming ever more difficult. Moral standards seem to totter; respect for things sacred is rare; self-serving absorption with individual well-being is everywhere. The teacher, whose task in part is to aid a student to fit into society, can scarcely help being aware of much in society he or she cannot recommend. Our news analysts are often our most prophetic voices to make us ethically aware in our world, but they are only part of a media world that tries to make morality out of popularity, judges right and wrong by monetary value, and rejects the values of the past to advocate "doing our thing" whether that "thing" is worth doing or not.

Teachers are only part of the team from which a child or youth absorbs values, but we are an important part. Especially at certain times in students' lives, teachers act as role models. If we have the courage to approach the values of our day critically, letting our students see where these values are inadequate and defeating, we are doing a real service. If we live unselfishly, with respect for what is life-enhancing and good, it will be more natural for our students to do so.

 Lord, in this mixed-up world help me to keep my sense of values straight and to pass healthy values on to my students. Amen.

Find an occasion to bring to your students some incident or word today that emphasizes what is honest and honorable in human behavior.

◼ THE SHARED RESPONSIBILITY

Prov. 4:1-19: "When I was only a little boy, my parents' only son, my father would teach me" (vv. 3-4).

Teachers should find Proverbs, especially chapters 1–4, encouragement for their sense of the importance of what they are doing. Wisdom, knowledge, learning, discernment, understanding, instruction—all these are given high priority. This is what in the Bible is called "wisdom literature," used by the wise men to teach the sons, the young men.

The wise men seem very aware of the importance of the involvement of parents in the education of their children. How well we as teachers know that too! Children from homes in which the development of knowledge and understanding is considered important will usually absorb much simply from intelligent conversation in their homes. Children from homes in which communication occurs in surly grunts and angry shouts absorb much too. All through their educational experiences, we are seeking either to reinforce the good the home has done or to overcome the hurdles the home has set up. We will be wise to pray for our students' homes and for ourselves, that we may relate to those we work with in a way that supplements with good what the home has already implanted in them.

 Lord, even in my ignorance of what their homes have or have not done for my students, make the guidance I give them relevant to their needs. Amen.

Do something today to communicate your pleasure in or your concern for a student to a parent who needs to become more involved.

■ WORDS OF TRUTH

Prov. 12:13-28:   "A lie has a short life, but truth lives on forever" (v. 19).

One of the demands of professional behavior is to treat our words with respect. The doctor, the lawyer, the psychologist, the priest or pastor, as well as the teacher or professor: all these must live with the knowledge that it is important that their words be used responsibly. If they are not, respect for the user as a professional is at stake. As Christian teachers we need to be doubly aware of the impact of our words lest we give offense.

I could hardly believe my ears when, as a high school teacher in a small community, I heard a new superintendent tell the assembled students, "I'm six-foot-three and 250 pounds, and if you think you're tough, I'm tougher!" They did—and he wasn't. He left at Christmas. Our words invite for us the respect or the lack of it from others. If by unwise and contentious words we walk through our days as teachers with a constant case of foot-in-mouth disease, we need to pray more that we may learn to guard our speech, to let our speech be placed under God's control. "Truthful lips" that are also kind are necessities for the Christian teacher who would keep her or his witness clear.

 Lord, set a guard before my lips today. Amen.

Try to restrain at least three impulsive but unwise statements that almost get past the door of your lips today.

■ TRUE COLLEGIALITY

Prov. 17:1-17: "If you want people to like you, forgive them when they wrong you. Remembering wrongs can break up a friendship" (v. 9).

Some suppose that they build themselves up when they tear someone else down. That is probably a common attitude in any type of work in which professional pride and skill are involved. If I treasure my ability to teach and know that my professional reputation rests in good part on that, admitting that a colleague teaches equally well or better is not easy. It is much easier to praise someone whose performance is quite unrelated to my own. Unfortunately, it is somehow also easy to suppose that we stand higher if we "repeat a matter" (KJV) and lower our competitor in the eyes of others.

A Christian attitude toward a colleague involves not only a willingness to give credit to him or her where that is due, but also a healthy confidence in our individual uniqueness, e.g., "Yes, she does this better than I do, but I do this well too." If two teachers exactly like me were available, my usefulness might be questioned. If there were two of him, he too would be replaceable. But God so fashioned matters that each of us is unique. That means each has something unique to offer, and we need not waste and mis-spend time tearing each other down.

Lord, give me confidence to believe in my own worth—and the willingness to recognize the worth and competence of others. Amen.

Watch for an occasion today to praise a colleague whom you are tempted to envy.

■ MY GOOD NAME

Prov. 21:28—22:12: "If you have to choose between a good reputation and great wealth, choose a good reputation" (22:1).

> Good name in man and woman, dear my lord,
> Is the immediate jewel of their souls: . . .
> . . . He that filches from me my good name
> Robs me of that which not enriches him,
> And makes me poor indeed.
>> Shakespeare's *Othello*,
>> act 3, scene 3, lines 155-161.

A good name is an important possession for a teacher, one that should be cherished and protected. What assures us of one? Few characteristics are as important in giving us a good name as fairness. A reputation for being fair is never so much discussed (except, perhaps, at a retirement party) as on that mythical but powerful student "grapevine" along which passes much information about teachers. We do well to guard carefully the kind of data that gets fed into that computer bank of unofficial student evaluation.

Not only we ourselves are concerned about our good names. Strange as it may seem, my reputation, when I am a Christian, has its effect on God's reputation in my community, my school, my classroom. My reputation for being fair is related to my living out of a belief in a God who is just. My integrity has a relationship to his faithful word to us. My good name is therefore to be guarded.

Lord, make me fair and honest and wise in my relationships with others today. Amen.

Find a way to do a little research on how your students evaluate you with regard to fairness.

■ LIVING DEFINITIONS

Prov. 23:29—24:7: "Don't be envious of evil people, and don't try to make friends with them" (24:1).

I was blessed in my education with many good teachers, many who "took heed" both to themselves and to their teaching, many who earned my respect as individuals as well as teachers. Two of these teachers were especially significant in my life, one in high school and one in college. They gave me so much—in friendship as well as in classes. I learned more about how to teach from their example than from any methods class. I followed their steps into the profession. My spiritual life matured as a result of their encouragement.

You might have already heard of the boy who, when asked to define the term *Christian,* said, "I can't define the word very well, but I know because my father is one." I knew what a Christian teacher was because my teachers Marie and Frida were such. I wonder what my former students remember about me—and yours about you? Paul calls us all, not only the young, to "be an example for the believers in your speech, your conduct, your love, faith, and purity" (1 Tim. 4:12). That is a big assignment for any of us today. If we complete it well, one day our students may rise up and call us blessed.

Lord, you who are the great example, make us fit examples for our students to follow. Amen.

Write a note of appreciation to one of your teachers who helped you know what a Christian is because he or she was one.

■ KEEPING OUR SECRETS

Prov. 25:1-12: "If you and your neighbor have a difference of opinion, settle it between yourselves and do not reveal any secrets" (v. 9).

In my early years of teaching, the mother of one of my students said to me, "I'm sure he tells you many things he never tells me." I wasn't convinced, because they had a beautiful mother-son relationship, but I have become aware that indeed young people do confide in teachers what they do not tell their parents. That is no insult to the parents. Young people are reaching out for independence; part of that is no longer sharing all things with parents. As teachers we are in a natural location to hear some of those confidences.

Keeping the confidence that someone has placed in us is very important. To violate such confidence is to destroy our ability to work effectively with that person. The young one who finds that such confidence has been breached by a teacher going to a parent will know better than to confide again, even if he needs an adult confidant.

What if we are told something that, without a doubt, the parents should know? The answer usually lies in counseling the young person to share the matter with the parents himself. Only in cases of clear and present danger should the trust shown in us be violated by our disclosing another's secret.

Lord, give me wisdom to handle with tact and grace what someone else confides in me. Amen.

Search your own memory for an instance when someone violated a confidence you had rested in them. Remember how you felt.

■ PROFESSIONAL ETHICS

Prov. 25:8-22: "Don't be too quick to go to court about something you have seen. If another witness later proves you wrong, what will you do then?" (v. 8).

The book of Proverbs could be the basis for an impressive code of ethics for almost any profession —certainly for teachers. Even in our brief section today, we are reminded of the importance of knowing the facts before we accuse, of respecting the privacy of confidences shared with us, of trustworthiness, of discretion, of honest testimony, and many other principles of behavior. It is not our perfect performance of these codes that makes us Christian, but as Christians we find in these codes much wisdom gleaned from the experience of others.

Many of our temptations to violate a code of professional ethics come from our very human desire to be "in the know." Every faculty has its gossips— those who can't wait to run from colleague to colleague with juicy tidbits of news which as often as not turn out to be false. Sometimes too there are those who foment discord as if they need it to give life interest, who even draw students into their squabbles with colleagues or administration. These attitudes are not appropriate for the Christian teacher. Better for us to provide words which are "like a design of gold, set in silver" (v. 11).

 Lord, grant that my observance of the ethics of my profession simply be a natural result of living according to your word. Amen.

Find a copy of a code of professional ethics for teachers and compare it with what the book of Proverbs advises.

■ RISKING THE FUTURE

Eccles. 2:12-26: "You work for something with all your wisdom, knowledge, and skill, and then you have to leave it all to someone who hasn't had to work for it" (v. 21).

The author of Ecclesiastes was a realist who found his realism quite uncomfortable. Searching for satisfaction, he looked to his possessions, his prestige, his public works. All of them were great. He had to admit that, now as old age crept up on him. But he also had to admit he was soon done with life, and these accomplishments would either disappear or be left behind to the control of some unappreciative fool. It was enough to make a person a cynic.

Like the author, we too, if we are realists, know that much of our effort to inspire students to be lovers of learning, to be intellectually curious, will be unsuccessful. Only with a minority do we really fulfil our yearning to produce students so motivated that they will continue to study, read, or ponder when they are on their own. Yet to surrender to cynicism, to accept that all our efforts go for nothing, is surely not the answer. Cynicism can poison our outlooks, stultify our growth, and ruin our joy. Cynicism does not build up; it tears down. Even if I have really inspired only two students in each year's class, that means for me 50 or 60 people who will serve society in their professions better than they would have otherwise. That would be well worth the effort.

Lord, make me content with what I can do rather than cynical about what I cannot do. Amen.

Take time to look back to note a student or two each year who really rejoiced your heart.

■ THE VOICE OF THE TEACHER

Isa. 30:15-26: ''. . . he [the Lord] himself will be there to teach you, and you will not have to search for him any more. If you wander off the road to the right or the left, you will hear his voice behind you saying, 'Here is the road. Follow it' '' (vv. 20-21).

How reassuring to have the promise that even though we "go through hard times" our eyes will see our teacher and his voice will be our guide! That is a promise that can make today not only livable but joyful.

Everyone knows the stereotype of the clown who stifles his weeping in order that he may bring pleasure to children. Teachers sometimes know the truth of that stereotype because they too may go about their work among their students with varied and personal problems that make it difficult for them to keep their minds on their subject matter. Sickness (their own or that of someone in their family), a tottering marriage, loneliness, care of aged parents, wayward children, financial problems—these concerns hover in the background as we make sure Johnny and Jane can read or learn geography.

God has given us no blanket assurance that the troubles of the world will pass us by because we are his children. But he has given us again and again the word that even in the midst of trouble he is present and near. Eventually our ears will hear him saying, "Here is the road. Follow it."

 Lord, I am grateful for the assurance that the day has come when I can see and hear you in the person of Jesus Christ, my Savior. Amen.

Memorize today's verse and repeat it to yourself during this day.

■ DON'T BLAME THE DEVIL

Jer. 8:4-12: ''They act as if my people's wounds were only scratches. 'All is well,' they say, when all is not well'' (v. 11).

The healing of a wound is a welcome event, and cannot happen too soon to please us. But there is a kind of healing which should better occur more slowly and deliberately. Many of us have probably experienced the kind of infection that sets in when a wound that has not been properly cleansed must eventually be opened again. God complains in our text that such superficial healing of moral infection which has not been dealt with is happening to his people. They are being told that all is well when there is deep trouble festering under the facade of outward peace.

We live in a society which attempts to cover over flagrant evil with rationalizations. A worthwhile book about that truth is Dr. Karl Menninger's *Whatever Happened to Sin?* We explain away sin as "understandable," "environmentally caused," or as illness. Or we say "The devil made me do it." True, many factors cause behavior, but we do our students no good when we encourage them to interpret their misdeeds as the fault of others or of society. Facing personal moral accountability is an important part of growing up.

Lord, help me to realize—and then to help my students to realize—the need to accept the responsibility for my own behavior. Amen.

Watch your own words today to squelch any false rationalizing of your motives.

■ A WORKING SENSE OF HUMOR

Jonah 3:10—4:11: "Then the Lord God provided a vine . . ." (4:6). "God provided a worm . . ." (4:7). "God provided a scorching east wind . . ." (4:8).

When I think back over the teachers I have known, often the ones I liked best were the ones with a lively sense of humor. I would almost say that a person with an inadequate sense of humor has no business in the classroom. The ability to see incongruities, even the ridiculous, in human behavior is essential to keeping a healthy perspective on life.

One famous teacher/student combination in the Bible is God and Jonah. Jonah's most serious problem was his lack of humor: he took himself too seriously when he was left with egg on his face. God, on the other hand, shows what from our point of view looks like a most useful sense of humor. To bring across the lesson to his prophet so fearful of losing face, God goes beyond the human to provide some unusual classroom aids—a plant, a worm, and a hot east wind. Jonah can hardly have escaped the lesson they taught, but there is never a shamefaced grin at his own sulkiness. There is only grumbling and a most ungracious resentment. No sense of humor at all!

Our sense of humor is as essential to our day in the schoolroom as our gradebooks. Without one, our grades as teachers are in jeopardy.

 Lord, keep me from taking myself so seriously that I lose my perspective on what is going on around me. Amen.

Tonight review the event of the day that you found most frazzling to your nerves and see if you can appreciate the humor in it.

■ GOD'S SILENCES

Hab. 1:12-17: "So why are you silent while they destroy people who are more righteous than they are?" (v. 13).

Habakkuk's question is one of those timeless, painful questions with which every thinking person struggles. There are many such questions, often having to do with suffering. How do we answer when faced with them?

One of the least helpful answers to a painful question is the pat, know-it-all, dogmatic kind. "God willed it that way," for example, in the face of a tragedy caused by human carelessness. "She brought it on herself," in the face of emotional illness. No one is as futile a comforter as the one who has all the explanations, all the answers, at tongue-tip.

The problem with such an attitude is that it omits the basis for the operation of the believer's whole rationale for life—faith. Luther drew his "The just live by faith" from our text. We appropriate the same answer when we go on bravely with a life that has major unanswered questions. God has never told us that he would supply the intellectual explanations for our problems in ready-made capsule form. He has promised us—and we can pass the word along to both students and colleagues alike—that he will never in the midst of those problems fail or forsake us.

Lord, help me to know better when people are hurting than to hand them pat answers. Amen.

Examine the pet phrases you use to comfort someone who is hurting. Are any of them pat answers you use to avoid the need to involve yourself with someone else's suffering?

■ WIELDING OUR INFLUENCE

Matt. 5:1-16:   "In the same way your light must
shine before people, so that they will see the good
things you do and praise your Father in heaven"
(v. 16).

We would find it quite amusing to look back at
the list of personal standards for teachers in the day
of our grandparents. Personal habits, dress, dating,
church attendance: all of these were prescribed for
public as well as for private school teachers. These
regulations, of course, were based on the awareness
that teachers were looked upon as models whose
behavior and appearance had influence with their
students.

While such regulations today are almost non-
existent, it is still true (almost unavoidably so) that
whether they like it or not, teachers are models
whose behavior influences others.

Most of us would probably prefer to be out from
under that kind of responsibility. Yet we know that
students of all ages are accumulating for themselves
habits and attitudes from a variety of sources, just
as we once did. What I am as a teacher, for instance,
has roots in what my best-liked teachers did and
were. As Christians, we see the responsibility as a
part of our opportunity to be models designed and
developed by Jesus Christ, controlled by him.
Wouldn't it be great to know that our students had
looked at us and grown to be like Jesus?

Lord, may those who look to me for a pattern
grow to be like you. Amen.

**Ask the Holy Spirit to make clear to you what in
your life could most easily become a negative
influence on others.**

■ THE LEFT CHEEK ALSO?

Matt. 5:38-48: "If anyone slaps you on the right cheek, let him slap the left cheek too" (v. 39).

A Christian's attitude toward violence often involves painful and bewildering decisions. Violence has not been divorced from education. In earlier years in some systems, the issue was often one of violence practiced by teachers in the disciplining of the students. The concern today is more often with the violence of the students toward the teachers. In the most dangerous systems, police patrol the halls of schools.

All the way down through history, humans—with some rare exceptions—have accepted violence as a means of enforcing the will of the powerful. The Palestine of Jesus' day was an illustration—Roman legions had swept through the land and conquered it. Yet into that time of military force and barbaric punishment, Jesus spoke the word that his followers were to choose the way of nonviolence. They were to turn the other cheek, to give up the coat as well as the cloak, to pray for forgiveness for those who persecuted them, even to love their enemies. Only then can the long tradition of violence be broken.

Do we believe that? Or are we ready—deliberately or unthinkingly—to perpetuate the long history of the violent response that in turn breeds multiplied violence in the future?

 Lord Christ, how bewildering and difficult is your command that we respond to violence with love! Help us to understand. Amen.

Find an occasion today for showing affection to someone whose actions in the past tempted you to respond violently.

◼ A LASTING REWARD

Matt. 6:1-6: "They love to stand up and pray in the houses of worship and on the street corners, so that every one will see them. I assure you, they have already been paid in full" (v. 5).

Those who seek an immediate reward, Jesus says, get just that. If that reward is instant popularity, they get it. But once having received that reward, they lose their claim on the heavenly reward, the eternal one.

There are times when as teachers we too must choose between instant favor with our students and favor which comes more slowly, favor that may not be realized for years. Teachers who seek instant popularity by giving high grades for mediocre performance may never know the honor and appreciation of the student who finds himself lacking the knowledge and skills that come with having to really study. Teachers who seek favor by giving only short and easy assignments may well find themselves forgotten by the time students realize their inadequate preparation for professional schools. Teachers who seek popularity by ridiculing what is sacred and praising what is cheap and profane may never know the reward of their students' respect.

We will surely find more satisfying the lasting reward that comes from our having high standards for both ourselves and our students.

 Lord, help me recognize the difference between instant popularity and that which comes from work well done. Amen.

Think back over your own education and note which teachers you remember with the greatest respect. What qualities won for them that respect?

■ ROOM TO BE ONESELF

Matt. 8:5-13:   "Oh no, sir," answered the officer. "I do not deserve to have you come into my house. Just give the order, and my servant will get well" (v. 8).

This centurion in our text, we can be sure, does not suggest to Jesus that he stay out of the centurion's house because he does not want him there. But he himself is used to getting results when he speaks to those under his command, and, recognizing the power there is in Jesus, he assumes that Jesus too can command and be obeyed. In this way he can save Jesus the embarrassment of entering the house of a Gentile, an act forbidden to a Jew.

It is interesting to note with what pleasure and commendation Jesus responds to the centurion's words, impressed with the man's faith and, no doubt, with his tact as well. He does not refuse aid to a Roman occupation officer. He gives the man room to be himself, recognizing the trust the man has placed in him and doing what is asked.

To give someone else—either student or colleague —room to be himself or herself, without pressing them into our mold or usual pattern of behavior, does not always come naturally to us; it does not satisfy our desire to order events. Jesus was a master of providing individuals with such openness and freedom. Are we?

 Lord, help me to recognize the things I do to pressure others into my mold rather than freeing them to be themselves. Amen.

Deliberately meet one request for advice today with the question, "Now how would it seem natural for you to decide this?"

■ THE PROCESS OF MATURING

Matt. 13:18-30:   "And the seeds sown in the good soil stand for those who hear the message and understand it: they bear fruit" (v. 23).

A pleasant event in teaching is meeting former students years later so we can see how they have matured. We knew them as children or young people. Since then they have become adults. We rejoice and feel pride in what they are doing, in their successes, in their contributions to church and community. The seed that has been sown has fallen on good ground and borne fruit. Perhaps we had not fully expected that, but it has happened.

How aware are we that in the same way good seed has been grown in the soil of our lives? As we can see the difference in our former students, so it should be possible for those who have known us in the past to see the maturing of our spiritual lives. Are we more loving than we were five years ago? Are our tempers under better control? Are we more knowledgeable students of the Word? Do we gossip less? Are we quicker to excuse others—to put the best construction on what someone else does? Can more of the mind of Christ be seen in us? These are fruits we too should be maturing for God's harvest.

Let the seed you have sown in my life mature, Lord, into a harvest that can glorify you. Amen.

Write a note or make a telephone call to a former teacher or pastor who would rejoice over your development since he or she last saw you.

■ TOUCHING

Matt. 14:28-36: "They begged him to let the sick at least touch the edge of his cloak; and all who touched it were made well" (v. 36).

Most of us can remember watching children clustering around their teacher, not satisfied till they have touched or been touched by her. The desire for closeness could be satisfied only by the physical touch. Often, as children grow older, they grow more shy about touching others—and children begin to go untouched not only at school but also at home.

Not all of us find touching others natural or easy, though usually it is easier with children or youth. And they need our touch. A touch says "I care about you. I like having you close to me." There are many who do not get that touch in their homes who need to get it from their teachers. Even college students still respond to being touched. A teacher in a Minnesota community college makes a point of hugging his students. He is called the "mad hugger," but his students respond with warmth and love in return.

Jesus was not slow to touch—children, sick people, those who crowded about him. With his touch came healing and love. We can pray that the Spirit can make us sensitive to the need of those we work with to be loved and healed by our touch.

Lord, make me a channel through which your love and healing touch may reach into the lives of my students. Amen.

Use an opportunity to touch a student who needs encouragement and warmth. Let that touch tell him or her of your real concern and affection.

■ LOSING FACE

Matt. 17:14-21: "Then the disciples came to Jesus in private and asked him, 'Why couldn't we drive the demon out?' " (v. 19).

How embarrassing! These very disciples had been among those sent out when Jesus had given them "authority to drive out evil spirits and to heal every disease and every sickness" (Matt. 10:1). That had been such an exalting experience and they returned glowing. Now, while Jesus and the inner circle had been up on the mountaintop, unavailable, a man with his epileptic son had come for healing and they had been unable to do a thing to help. Then Jesus had returned and done with such ease what they could not do at all. They could hardly wait to get Jesus alone and ask him the reason. Talk about losing face!

As teachers we have our worries, don't we, about losing face. A student asks a question and we set out to answer it in our usual confident way only to come to a sputtering halt, realizing that we do not know the answer. How do we handle that?

It is no crime to be less than omniscient. Jesus' disciples knew what they needed to do—they went to the Master for the answer. We too need to have the humility to admit that we do not know all things and be willing to set out on an honest search.

Lord, help me to be able to admit that I am not as knowledgeable as you. Amen.

Learn how to use your ignorance of a fact as a means of getting a student to set off in search of it.

■ RECORD KEEPING

Matt. 18:18-35:   "Lord, if my brother keeps on sinning against me, how many times do I have to forgive him? Seven times?" (v. 21).

In the Bible, seven is the symbolic number of fullness, completeness. Peter no doubt believed he was being generous in his suggestion of seven as the acceptable number of times an offending brother need be forgiven. Imagine his surprise when the Master responds with a figure intended to be the equivalent of "always." Paul, in his magnificent and psychologically perceptive depiction of love in 1 Corinthians 13, agrees. Love does not "keep account of evil"; it "does not keep a record of wrongs."

How wonderful it would be if school buildings were places of ideal behavior with no need for the practice of forgiveness! Unfortunately, our memories of offenses are often longer than the longest corridors in the building. "I won't forget that she voted against me on that decision." "I'll never forget how that boy embarrassed me in front of the principal." "She volunteered just to make me look bad." "I would have gotten merit pay if it hadn't been for him." All sorts of accusations come from students, colleagues, and administrators.

How close does the number come to 490? There's still a long way to go. And there is still hope that we will learn we hurt ourselves more seriously with our record keeping than we do anyone else.

 Lord, there is one kind of accountant I don't want to be—one who keeps record of wrongs. Please let me be free from that. Amen.

If there is any hidden grudge between you and anyone at school, do something today to clear it up.

■ INSPECTOR COMING

Matt. 24:32-50: "Watch out, then, because you do not know what day your Lord will come" (v. 42).

Things are likely different now than when I began to teach—of course they are! Our superintendent was notified days in advance of the coming of the school inspectors. There would be plenty of time to have the plan books filled in, records updated, and the building sparkling. One could easily get the impression that what mattered was not regular performance but having all in order when the inspector came. It was doubtless one way to get things done—at least once a year.

Would we act in a similar way if we could know the unknowable, the day of the Lord's return? Would we scramble through a few days of cleaning out the litter in our lives, of readying our report of good intentions? Would we grab the opportunities for getting loving words spoken, some appropriate apologies made, and expressions of appreciation uttered?

If those things would become important if we knew his coming was imminent, perhaps this is just the time to do them. How do we know it is *not*? If they are ever to be done, perhaps this is the only time. Even if he is not coming just now, aren't those just the things we should be doing at all times?

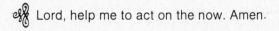 Lord, help me to act on the now. Amen.

Make a list of three "I should" acts for today. Change them to "I will" and get at least two of them done today.

■ OFF ON A TANGENT

Mark 5:21-34:   "She had heard about Jesus, so she came in the crowd behind him, saying to herself, 'If I just touch his clothes, I will get well,' " (vv. 27-28).

Jesus was on his way to Jairus' house to raise a child from the dead—an urgent mission. Yet he took time to discover who in a crowd had touched him in faith. He could have said, "Don't distract me now. I'm doing something important. I have a plan for this day and must hold to it."

As teachers we know our plans for the day are important. We have experience with students whose questions or comments lead us off on tangents. Like Jesus, we need to evaluate the importance of the tangent, and, if it is worthy, to be flexible enough to deal with it without getting sidetracked. When Jesus had reassured the woman, he continued on to Jairus' house.

Students sometimes make a game out of getting teachers so sidetracked they never get back on the main track of the lesson. Some of these tangents may bear fruit—but likely only a few. We need to differentiate between times when it is important to stay with the topic planned and times when the tangent opens up an opportunity to feed a genuine desire to learn, to clear up a misunderstanding, or to meet a timely vital need. Jesus did.

 Lord, give me a sense of perspective about what is important and what is simply a wandering away from the subject. Amen.

Anticipate some worthwhile tangent that has a relation to the life of your students today and make an enjoyable moment out of it for them.

■ THE MASTER TEACHER

Mark 6:30-44: "So he began to teach them many things" (v. 34).

When we go to our classrooms, we do the same kind of work on which our Lord spent much of his time and effort in his earthly life. He was a teacher —a master teacher. Studying the Gospels to examine Jesus' role as a teacher can be a rewarding methods course, with insights we can put to work in our own activities.

Jesus responded as a teacher to the crowds he perceived as "sheep without a shepherd." He set out to replace ignorance with understanding. He knew the value of simple object lessons. His parables were memorable and clear—lost sheep, lost sons, lost coins, seed on stony ground. When he had illuminated a truth, he encouraged his listeners to act on it: "Go thou, and do likewise." He made use of the developments of the immediate moment to draw unforgettable lessons. The disciples' attempt to protect him from the intrusions of children on his time resulted in a great lesson on priorities. His words were backed up by his example. Always there was acceptance of the individual with a need—an acceptance coupled with love, and without a judgmental attitude.

If we approach our teaching using these "methods," we will be outstanding teachers.

Lord, help me as a teacher to fit my feet into your steps. Amen.

Take time today to read Luke 9:46—19:27, noting especially Jesus' techniques as a teacher.

■ SENDING THEM ON

Luke 8:26-39: "The man from whom the demons had gone out begged Jesus, 'Let me go with you.' But Jesus sent him away" (v. 38).

How easy to sympathize with the man in this story who, freed from the terror and loneliness of his condition, pleaded to remain with Jesus. If only he could stay with this one who set him free! There must have been real disappointment in his heart when Jesus refused his plea to be part of his company. "Go back home and tell what God has done for you," Jesus said.

While what we as teachers can do for others is not likely to be anywhere near as marvelous as what Jesus did for this man, teachers sometimes do know the experience of having students respond so positively to their approach and personality that they become too emotionally attached, and they prefer to lean on that relationship rather than go on to become more independent and mature. It is not our purpose to collect our own personal cheering section or coterie. Since such attachment can be flattering, it may be difficult for teachers to do as Jesus did and send such students on their way to the next instructor. But that is better than to allow them to fasten themselves with unhealthy dependence on us.

Lord, help me to avoid binding my students to me in an unhealthy way. Amen.

Take time to examine your relationships with your students to make sure that you are not contributing to someone's becoming a leaner.

■ RECEIVING THIS CHILD

Luke 9:46-48: "Whoever welcomes this child in my name, welcomes me; and whoever welcomes me, also welcomes the one who sent me. For he who is least among you all is the greatest" (v. 48).

To welcome a child in Jesus' name is to welcome not only the child but the Father. And to receive the child and the Father's blessing is usually also to receive the love of the child—a very precious gift.

One of the prized serendipities of teaching comes in those moments when a child or young person turns to us with spontaneous affection and desire to share with us: the kindergarten child who must hug his teacher right now; the elementary child whose eyes glow when she is allowed to help her teacher in some way; the high school student who talks for days about the experiment she worked on with her teacher; the college student who, along with a late paper, shares an awed account of the birth the night before of his baby. As we welcome them, and with them God's blessing, we also experience the joy of sharing their lives in some precious moments.

Teachers have ready access to knowing that "he who is least among you all is the greatest." Others may call people great as they go on to win their medals in the adult world. We know that there already was greatness in them—the great value that God places upon them.

 Lord, open my eyes to see additional ways in which I can welcome in your name the students with whom I work today. Amen.

Say to yourself several times today as you face your classes, "I welcome each one of you in Jesus' name."

■ A PROPER MODESTY

Luke 14:7-14: "For everyone who makes himself great will be humbled, and everyone who humbles himself will be made great" (v. 11).

Whether we are aware of it or not, most of us have a little collection of devices ready for use in letting others know the things we have done which have gone unrecognized or unappreciated. Perhaps that is good. We deserve credit for what is done well. Most of the time, though, we do best to let others sound our praises, or to remain silent. We can turn our attention to making someone else feel appreciated and included.

What a flip-flop there would be in the social circles of our land if Jesus' advice to save our invitations for those who have no way to repay us were followed! No longer would there be dinner guests grumbling they would rather stay home and watch television. Instead there would be a fine dinner for those whose treats are few and limited in scope— and God left to present the awards.

We need not deny our good works. They are tasks we ought to be doing. But we do not need to be panicked into proclaiming our own. If others do not find out, and if our merit pay or advancement is slow to arrive, we can remember that "God will repay you on the day the good people rise from death" (v. 14). In the meantime, let's leave our praise for others to sing.

Lord, let me be content to let others give me praise rather than to advertise my claims to it myself. Amen.

Find occasion today to praise some act or quality of another teacher on your floor.

■ FOCUS ON INDIVIDUALS

Luke 19:1-10:   ''When Jesus came to that place, he looked up and said to Zacchaeus, 'Hurry down, Zacchaeus, because I must stay in your house today' '' (v. 5).

The time had come. Jesus set his face toward Jerusalem, the danger and opposition reckoned with. Nothing would turn him away from that journey, that rendezvous with the Father's will. His confrontation with the powers of evil would not be avoided. Yet before he and his associates travel farther than Jericho, his progress is halted—for a hated tax collector perched ludicrously in a tree. With his great appointment to keep in Jerusalem, why stop for thieving Zacchaeus?

Jesus' response to Zacchaeus is typical of him. No matter how great the numbers, the seeking individual gets attention. Zacchaeus' tree climbing is evidence of his desire to meet Jesus. The Master will stop in the dense crowd to ask "Who touched me?" when an individual asks healing. The one whose need is immediate comes first.

How similar to Jesus' attitude is ours toward one child, one young person? Is he or she an interruption we must tolerate, a nuisance when we have other things to do, a clod we have to spend time on that could be better spent on our brighter students? If we would be followers of the Great Teacher today, the individual seeking us out must be put first.

 Lord, help me never to lose sight of the individual in my task of working with a group. Amen.

Reminisce a bit about how being recognized as an individual influenced your response to your teachers.

■ THE POWER OF PRAYER

Luke 22:24-34: "But I have prayed for you, Simon, that your faith will not fail" (v. 32).

Most of us have no doubt read reports of experiments which claim that prayer has made plants grow more rapidly. Whether we have been convinced or not, we can believe that there is a power in prayer that goes beyond our ability to explain. It is offered to us in those great promises of Christ. "When you pray and ask for something, believe that you have received it, and you will be given whatever you ask for" (Mark 11:24). From the amount of attention to prayer in the Bible—and the amount of the Bible made up of recorded prayer—we can know we are dealing with power far beyond our own. Prayer changes not only things, but people.

What a privilege to invoke this power for good on behalf of our students! What could it mean if a teacher with 30 students prayed for them by name each day? What might result if I spend the 20 minutes my students take to write a quiz talking to God about each of them? (There's no forbidding that kind of prayer in schools!) Love and concern on our part meeting the love and power of the Father on their behalf could bring real blessings into their lives. It's worth a try.

 Lord, keep me aware that one of the most effective things I can do for my students is to bring them to you in prayer. Amen.

Make use of your gradebook today in bringing your students before God for his blessing.

◼ FRIENDSHIP FOR SALE

Luke 23:1-12: "On that very day Herod and Pilate became friends; before this they had been enemies" (v. 12).

The saying "Politics makes strange bedfellows" finds clear illustration in this perverse friendship between Pilate and Herod. They already had similarities: both were ambitious, eager for Rome's favor. Now they had another characteristic in common: each wanted to get Jesus off his hands without having to make a decision about him. Pilate, hearing Jesus was a Galilean, gleefully sent him off to Herod, believing he had avoided the uncomfortable trap set for him. Let that "fox" make the decision! Herod is glad to have his curiosity about Jesus satisfied, but he is not about to get involved in any unpopular decisions. Let Pilate take care of his own problems. As a result of their sharing of the problem, the procurator and the puppet king become friends.

New friendships are a welcome addition to our professional lives. But if those new friendships form as a result of negative aspects of our associations, out of a common desire to evade responsibility, or a desire to see another teacher put down, we might remember the strange friendship between Pilate and Herod and seek to be sure our friendships have a more positive basis.

 Lord, thank you for new friendships. May they have a common basis in our love for you, not in our attempt to use each other. Amen.

Think through your friendships to make sure that you are not being used to support someone else's political maneuverings.

■ A LOOK AT POTENTIAL

John 4:7-30: ". . . but whoever drinks the water that I will give him will never be thirsty again" (v. 14).

One of the fascinating aspects of Jesus' dealing with persons is the way he goes beyond what an individual *is* to appeal to what that individual might *become*. The impulsive, foot-in-mouth fisherman can become Peter, the rock. John, son of thunder, can become the apostle of love. The demoniac among the tombs can be set free to be Jesus' witness to his hometown people.

What a comforting challenge for each of us to know that God works with us in our lives not according to what we have been or even what we are, but by what he knows we, by his grace, can become. Our whole Christian life is a process of becoming what he knows we can be.

How do we look at our students? Do we see them in terms of what they are, or of what they have the potential to become? We need to keep visualizing them positively, in the light of what they can become in the future if our work with them is successful. If our mental image of a student is a negative one, we need to change it lest we become the kind of influence that reinforces the negative in his or her life.

 Gracious Spirit of God, thank you for seeing in me something worth your continued presence and work in my life. Amen.

Work today to change the image you carry of students you have who seem least likely to succeed. Visualize them in terms of what, given your help and God's, they could become.

■ STOOPING TO SERVE

John 13:1-17: "Then he poured some water into a washbasin and began to wash the disciples' feet and dry them with the towel around his waist" (v. 5).

No wonder Peter is perturbed when he sees Jesus begin to wash the feet of his disciples in that Upper Room prepared for the Passover Feast. That was servants' work, surely not appropriate for him whom Peter had earlier identified by saying, "Thou art the Christ, the son of the living God." Christ to wash Peter's feet?

All of us, like Christ in the story, know there are tasks to be done for which people seldom volunteer. We teachers can make lists of undesirable tasks in our profession too, can't we! There are the necessary but unexciting committees that must have members— and secretaries. There are the supplies that must be counted and the lunch moneys to be collected. We'd rather not be bothered by our turn to sell tickets, and why should it be our job to straighten an untidy room?

If we had watched that scene in the Upper Room, what would that experience have done to our willingness to do the menial tasks of our days? If our Lord could wash the tired, dirty feet of his disciples, then it is not for me to refuse the humble chores that are involved in my daily service for him.

Lord, forgive my pride and egocentricity. Make me willing to stoop to serve as you did. Amen.

Go out of your way at least three times today to pick up refuse without waiting for the custodian to do it.

■ EVEN GREATER THINGS

John 14:1-13: "Whoever believes in me will do what I do—yes, he will do even greater things, because I am going to the Father" (v. 12).

To grapple with Jesus' statement that his disciples will do "greater things" than he did is to face a real challenge in our spiritual lives. How ever could that be? He healed the sick, raised the dead, drove out demons, taught the ignorant. How can we ever do "greater things"? The greatest work we can do will leave us humble because we know that it has been done only by his enabling.

Almost all teachers at some time have the humbling experience of realizing we have in class a student whose intelligence and perceptiveness goes beyond our own. It is easy then to feel personally threatened, to feel that it would be better for him or her to stay with the pace of the slower students, to fear questions that might show us up, to let that student be bored because we do not want to take extra effort to keep such a student challenged.

How much better if we can look at that student, bright with potential that may take him or her far beyond us, and rejoice that we can have a part in teaching and guiding one who will do greater things than we! Rather than be jealous, we can be thrilled when that student excels.

Lord, keep me from ever being resentful of the intelligence or success of my students. Amen.

Find the opportunity today to challenge and show appreciation of the student whose level of ability could seem threatening to you as a teacher.

■ YELLOW NOTE CARDS

John 15:1-17: "My Father's glory is shown by your bearing much fruit; and in this way you become my disciples" (v. 8).

Joking about the professor whose lecture notes have turned yellow with age is common among teachers. Many institutions have recently changed from teachers' colleges to state colleges to state universities. Students have spotted final examinations and syllabi which have continued for several years to bear the old school name. They have suspected— probably rightly—that the tests and syllabi were old ones, work-avoiders for the professor.

Teachers at every level of education face their own kinds of challenges in changing an easy class preparation for one that is fresh, updated, and adapted specifically for the group of students to be taught. It is not hard to know which kind of preparation will bear the fruit of knowledge and needed skills for the student. The fresh preparation takes time and effort, but don't we feel better about ourselves when we have produced it?

To be the best teacher I know how to be is my responsibility as a Christian. In that activity I grow and bear fruit and can be known as one of the followers of the Great Teacher. To bear a Christian witness and to be a lazy teacher do not fit together. Before long, that witness will suffer.

Lord, keep me today from taking easy ways out rather than fruit-producing ones. Amen.

Throw away one lesson plan for tomorrow and prepare it with a fresh, more productive approach.

■ THE PROBABILITY OF PERSECUTION

John 15:18-25: "If they persecuted me, they will persecute you too; if they obeyed my teaching, they will obey yours too" (v. 20).

We can easily assume that, because we are Christians seeking to do our work in a spirit of love and good will, others will look at us with a glow of approval, and interpersonal relationships will be one happy song. Perhaps that will be true if we come across simply as "nice" people. But if our lives demonstrate those aspects of Christianity that result from radical obedience to Jesus' commands, we may well meet some of the persecution he met. Behavior that brought him criticism and opposition in his days on earth still rouses criticism and disapproval today.

Do you find that hard to believe? If so, watch what happens when you become the unofficial advocate in your school for those from a minority group your community considers a nuisance. What happens if you insist on total openness and honesty on controversial issues? Or what happens if your convictions cross those of a heated majority and you insist on remaining true to them in an important vote?

We can live persecution-free lives, but only if we avoid making our decisions by Christ's standards when expediency and popularity call us to follow the herd.

Lord, give me the courage to live by your standards, and sensitivity to rightly discern that which they demand from me. Amen.

Find occasion today to befriend a colleague whose actions have offended others on your faculty.

■ THE SEARCH FOR TRUTH

John 18:28-38: "And what is truth?" Pilate asked (v. 38).

Is the world a result of the creative act of God or of chance? Are human beings essentially good, or is the Bible right when it says, "There is no one who is righteous"? Can humans surmount their problems by their own powers? Are we our brothers' keepers, or is "enlightened selfishness" our best economic policy?

If we as teachers listen, sooner or later we hear our students ask Pilate's question: What is truth? What help can we give them as they encounter the difficult questions that shake their faith in what they have been taught at home and church? In a public school can we give our own answers? Have we found our own answers yet?

I am grateful for both public school and church college teachers who emphasized for me that all truth belongs to God. As human beings, we come to understand that truth one piece at a time. We may change our ideas of what that truth is as we discover more and more of the evidence available both in Scripture and in the universe—both human and physical. But even where we are in doubt, God's truth stands firm. Our confidence in that reality can be a reassurance to our students, even without our seeking to indoctrinate them with our own beliefs.

God of all truth, may my confidence in you as the source of all truth be evident from my attitudes even when I must refrain from indoctrination. Amen.

Say something in your classes today to indicate your deep respect for truth.

■ THE CONTAGIOUS CHRIST

Acts 4:1-20: "The members of the Council were amazed to . . . learn that they were ordinary men of no education. They realized then that they had been companions of Jesus" (v. 13).

No doubt there was quite an obvious difference between the learned men of the Sanhedrin and Peter and John, even if the disciples no longer wore their fishing clothes. As the rulers and the elders listened to these Galileans, they must have been impressed at the poise and courage of these uneducated backwoodsmen. Fishermen, even if they were businessmen in a way, didn't often face rulers and elders. Yet here were these men, untroubled by the reproofs showered upon them. The big man, especially, talked to them as if he were an equal. How could this be?

Their explanation was an interesting one. These men had obviously been with that other Galilean called Jesus, and that troublesome serenity of his in the face of trial before the Sanhedrin rubbed off on these men too. He had, truly, something contagious about him.

What do people among whom we work and fraternize decide about us as a result of our speech and our serenity in the face of disagreement or stress? How satisfying if their response too would be to take note of the fact we have been with Jesus.

Lord, may your likeness more and more be seen in my daily life. Amen.

Send a note of appreciation to someone whose Christ-likeness has been a blessing in your life.

■ USING THE RIGHT TACK

Acts 17:16-34: "Paul stood up in front of the city council and said, 'I see that in every way you Athenians are very religious' " (v. 22).

While we recognize Jesus as the Master Teacher, Paul ranks high in teaching ability too. His appearance before the Athenian Greeks on Mars Hill is a superb example of a good teacher at work, one who knows just how to reach out to those who are ignorant of or even hostile to his message. He begins by complimenting them on their interest in religious things (he could have called them heathen). He begins with what they know (the altar to the unknown god) and moves from the familiar to the unfamiliar (Jesus and his resurrection). He gives them a reason for accepting the God of whom he speaks (that God is the universal Creator, no private possession interested only in Christians or Jews). He quotes their own poets to them. There is no condescending, no belittling, no claim of superiority on his part.

How easy it is to turn others off by the manner and the introduction we use when we seek to teach! The condescending attitudes, the superiority we imply, our tactlessness can effectively close the ears of our students. Both Paul and Jesus in their teaching were honest and open in confronting others, but their tact and love also are evident. Better examples we cannot have!

Lord, teach me how to approach others tactfully and effectively. Amen.

Practice applying some technique used by Jesus or Paul today to the class toward which you feel the least interest.

■ CONSISTENCY—WHAT KIND?

Rom. 2:1-11: "But you, my friend, do these very things for which you pass judgment on others! Do you think you will escape God's judgment?" (v. 3).

A foolish consistency," says Emerson, "is the hobgoblin of little minds, adored by little statesmen, philosophers, and divines." Perhaps of teachers too. We all know people who can abide no change, for whom every detail of the day must be a round peg which without fail fits into a round hole. If something about a student or a colleague's behavior threatens to upset that consistency, their whole day is thrown out of focus. "We've always done it that way!" There is a kind of consistency that traps people in prisons of their own making.

But there is also a kind of consistency that is wise and necessary. That is the kind involved in holding up for myself the same standards as I demand from other people. If I excuse white lies in my own speaking, can I criticize them in others? If I justify my own loss of temper, can I blame the student who loses his? If I decide not to meet a class on a scheduled day, why should I be critical of the student who cuts?

There is a foolish consistency that grows into rigidity which we would do well to avoid. But there is also a wise consistency which keeps us fair to others and able to respect ourselves.

Lord, help me not to demand more from others than I am willing to demand from myself. Amen.

Print the words of the prayer above on the cover of your gradebook where you will see them often.

■ WITNESSES UNTO ME

Rom. 10:5-15:   "If you confess that Jesus is Lord and believe that God raised him from death, you will be saved" (v. 9).

Christian teachers disagree on the freedom of a teacher to witness to his or her own faith in the public classroom. Some believe one is totally free to witness by word; others believe that in a pluralistic society a Christian has only the same right to witness by word in the classroom as does a teacher who is a Buddhist or a Moslem. The issue can be theoretical in a small community in which the only religion is Christian. It can be very real in a community of varied religious backgrounds.

Each of us as teachers must find the answer he or she can live with that is true to the individual situation. There is a witness of life that is never out of place. There is a witness of word that is appropriate when we are asked for our personal beliefs. There is a witness of fairness—we are as free to witness in favor of faith as nonbelieving teachers are to speak against it. There is a witness open in out-of-school contacts with students. There is a sense in which the public school classroom is not the place to use a captive audience for purposes of evangelizing. But if the witness of life is attractive, the witness of words will find a place.

Lord, may your Spirit be my guide in letting my witness to my faith in you be tactful and constant. Amen.

Keep a Testament or Bible on your classroom or office desk as a witness to the importance you give to it.

■ VALUING THE GIFTS

Rom. 12:3-8:   "So we are to use our different gifts in accordance with the grace that God has given us" (v. 6).

In several of the towns in which I have taught, I have felt sorry for students—especially boys—who were not outstanding athletes. Perhaps there were other schools in which the pedestal of honor was reserved only for talented musicians or for exceptional scholars. But where I was present to observe, pity the boy who was too short, too lightweight, or uncoordinated. Only the leftovers of attention were his. Until recently, the girls' only hope was a place on the cheering squad. Fortunately, in most schools these unfair emphases are changing.

Youngsters with talents that differ need to be given encouragement to develop the gifts they have, not to be set aside while we give our praises to the achievers in the area a teacher or a community most admires. The ones who haven't found their talents yet have a special need to be helped to see what their gifts are. And the one who seems to be without a special gift needs to be shown the most love of all. The gift of being loving, friendly, and sympathetic is often the precious possession of the retarded child—provided someone has taken care of developing that gift. How important that we be fair and impartial in the value we place on the talent an individual has, rather than on the unachievable one he yearns for!

Lord, you who have given us gifts, make us developers of those gifts. Amen.

Give a sincere compliment to a student who needs to grow in confidence to use the gift he or she has.

■ RESPECT FOR AUTHORITY

Rom. 13:1-10:   "Pay, then, what you owe them;
pay them your personal and property taxes, and
show respect and honor for them all" (v. 7).

Perhaps because we are used to exerting a good
deal of command in our classes, teachers do not
find it easy to yield to authority. In honesty we
must admit that some of the frictions within
education come from an unwillingness to submit
to a system when we are confident that we are as
competent to make the decisions as our administrators
are. And if we are educated to a high level of
expertise, we have few qualms about asserting
our opinions about how things should be done.

Paul surely had the position and the prestige in
the early church to have insisted on preeminence.
Also, in a time of corrupt rule and misrule, we might
have expected him to be full of criticism of and
warnings to corrupt rulers. Instead Paul admonishes
the Roman Christians, many of whom were slaves
who might have been incited to rebellion, to pay
honor and respect where those were due and taxes as
required. If, in that kind of society, God expected
obedience to properly constituted authority, perhaps
we need to think twice and be sure of our own
motives if we set students the example of proud
resistance to necessary controls.

 Lord, I have a bad habit of thinking I know
almost all of the answers. Help me to be
confident without being arrogant. Amen.

**In some dispute about decisions today, deliberately
defend (at least temporarily) the administrative
position to force yourself to really look at what its
reasons are.**

■ SIMPLY GOD'S SERVANTS

1 Cor. 3:1-11:   "After all, who is Apollos? And who
is Paul? We are simply God's servants, by whom
you were led to believe" (v. 5).

Sometimes it must have been hard for Paul to control
the feeling that those churches he had established,
often in the face of extreme opposition, were his in a
unique way. When some looked upon Apollos as
their spiritual father, how easy it would have been
for Paul to resent such disloyalty to himself, to be
bitter that he had to keep reminding believers in
those churches of his credentials. But then came the
knowledge of how futile the planting and the
watering of spiritual seed by any human sower if
God were not active to give the growth.

I have had a frustrating student in class this year—
what a joy he has been! I cannot take credit for
anything except providing opportunities for him to
write. Other teachers before me have helped him
develop a fine set of skills. He is intelligent,
motivated, conscientious. He is a constant reminder
that much of the credit for progress my students
show does not belong to me. Like Paul, I must be
grateful to be a part of the planting and the
watering, and aware that to take credit for the
harvest is something about which I must be
very modest.

Lord, thank you for many good teachers whose
work makes my work more successful. Amen.

**Find an occasion to recognize the good work a
previous teacher has done with one of your best
students.**

■ HANDLING THE GRAY AREAS

1 Cor. 10:11—11:1: "I try to please everyone in all that I do, not thinking of my own good, but of the good of all, so that they might be saved" (10:33).

One of the hardest lessons in growing to maturity is to realize that in ethical decisions there are few simple choices between black and white but many between variegated shades of gray. Small children and even some adults try to live in a two-tone moral world. Paul in our text is too much of a realist to suppose all moral behavior can be decided on such simplistic terms.

Children expect to be able to decide between black and white. Adolescence is full of confrontations in which such decisions are not possible. Even as adults we keep meeting situations in which shades of gray are almost indistinguishable. In aiding a young person faced with such decisions, a teacher may be of most assistance when he or she does not over-simplify the problem and try to return the student to a choice between black and white. Our students need to know that all our lives long these decisions call us to careful thought and prayer—prayer for guidance about what is right in specific cases, and also prayer that God's Spirit develop in us a moral sensitivity that will remain with us throughout life. As teachers we have an influence on moral growth; we cannot excuse ourselves by saying we teach only facts.

Lord, give me a moral sensitivity that will keep me from harming others by overly simplistic judgments. Amen.

Watch for a natural opportunity to point out to your students the complexity that may be present in moral decisions.

■ A LESSON IN APPRECIATION

1 Cor. 12:12-31: "And so there is no division in the body, but all its different parts have the same concern for one another" (v. 25).

The members of the early church had many lessons to learn. Paul strives diligently to help them cultivate the right attitudes. One thing he emphasizes is their need to recognize the worth of those whose role in the Christian community is different from their own. Their operation as the body of Christ demands that each be willing to give honor, love, and recognition to the others.

There is a logical transfer from that situation to our life within a school. We teachers are not the only ones present. We need to recognize and accept the value of the cook and the custodian, the secretary and the social worker, the counselor and the principal as well as our own. It is easy to believe, because learning is the essential function, that our role is the only one to be served. Students may learn much from the conscientiousness of the custodian or the compassion of the school nurse which complements the lessons we teach. As Christians, we are to see in others the same worth we possess, to support, to encourage, to befriend. It is not our place to say to another, "I don't need you."

 Lord, give me a truly democratic spirit, ready to see and acknowledge the worth in others. Amen.

Go out of your way today to express your appreciation for someone who serves a different role from yours in your school.

■ A MORE EXCELLENT WAY

1 Corinthians 13: "I may be able to speak in the languages of men and even of angels, but if I have no love, my speech is no more than a noisy gong or a clanging bell" (v. 1).

I have fond memories of a student who often, once school was out, the buses pulled away, and I settled in at my desk to prepare for the next day, would carefully empty my wastebasket, turn it upside down, and sit down on it to secure all my attention. Otherwise he went home to an empty house for those after-school hours. It was better to stay where he had an audience, someone to show him affection.

Teachers know something of the endless amounts of love students can absorb. Those loved at home know the joys of being loved and come for more. Those who are loved but seldom shown that love openly come too. Those who know little love are shy about giving signs that they too would like some, thank you. And we? Of course we want some as well.

Paul's definition of love fits the schoolroom well. "Love is patient and kind; . . . not jealous . . . not ill-mannered . . . or irritable . . . is happy with the truth. . . . Love is eternal." Where do we get the abundant supply we need if we are to give it? We can ourselves be made into unclogged channels for the love of God, which has already blessed us, to move through.

 Thank you, Lord, for the love that can pour from you through me to others, especially to my students. Amen.

Find at least three occasions today to tell a student "I really like you!"—and mean it.

■ SPIRITUAL SELF-TESTING

2 Cor. 13:1-7: "Put yourselves to the test and judge yourselves, to find out whether you are living in faith" (v. 5).

Most of us teachers by now have made use of the kind of testing in which a student can put down an answer and then immediately be shown the correct answer—some method of self-testing. That's what Paul tells these Christians they are to do continually—self-examination. They are to do this not to discover their intellectual progress or to find a malignant tumor, but to assure themselves that their faith is alive and well, that Christ indwells them with his spiritual force. "The Christ you have to deal with is not a weak person outside you, but a tremendous power inside you" (v. 3, Phillips).

Powerful as this presence is within us, we can lose the sense of his presence if we take him for granted, if we let our faith grow torpid. We puzzle sometimes over how a child can become so separated from its family that in minutes he or she is lost and search parties must set out. If we do not have a self-testing program, we may fail to realize that Christ is no longer active in us and thus fail to meet the test. He will not leave us as long as we desire his presence.

 Lord, as I examine myself, may I find ever-constant evidence of your presence in my life. Amen.

Formulate a set of five questions appropriate for spiritual self-examination. Keep them in your Bible for ready reference.

■ UPHOLDING THE TRUTH

2 Cor. 13:5-13: "For we cannot do a thing against the truth, but only for it" (v. 8).

Serious observers of our society are aware that the practice of truth is sadly lacking in the lives and speech of many today. Evidently there is no compulsion to do nothing "against the truth."

Teachers hardly need to be told that. Education is as full of problems related to truth as any other profession, whether it be cheating on exams, buying of research papers, padding recommendations, gossip in the faculty lounge, falsifying a grade to keep an athlete eligible, or administrative decisions made in violation of open meeting laws. Even teachers who disapprove of certain dishonest acts (e.g., students cheating) are not always honest about the necessity of their own absences.

Honesty is difficult in any society. We adjust to realities of our situations by lies so white that they seem on the borderline of truth. We use gobbledygook to avoid telling an unpleasant truth—"Billy has a peer-adjustment problem" instead of "Billy likes to beat up on smaller children." A tape of a day's worth of our own conversation might horrify us with the number of evasions of truth of which we are unaware.

As a Christian teacher, I have a responsibility to the truth cannot avoid. To fulfill it will not be easy.

Lord, tune my ear to your standards of truth. Help me not to do "a thing against the truth." Amen.

Listen to yourself and those around you with extra care for a day. What instances of disregard for truth do you discover?

■ COLOR US GREEN

Gal. 5:13-26: "But if you act like wild animals, hurting and harming each other, then watch out, or you will completely destroy one another" (v. 15).

We must not be proud or irritate one another or be jealous of one another." How would that be for a motto to hang in the faculty lounge? Probably teachers are no more likely to act like wild animals than are people in other professions. But those of us who have been in education for any length of time, particularly at certain levels, do not need to be told that jealousy among colleagues is one of our most common professional sins. If you question that, try being the one who gets merit pay when the majority of your colleagues do not, or the one who is promoted when few promotions are given. The gossip in the coffee lounge offers ample opportunities for us to cut down the teacher who had our class the year before or to ridicule the teacher who volunteers to do more than the majority feels called upon to do.

Christian teachers will find it just as tempting as others to give demeaning reasons why some teachers are so loved by students, to assume that teachers who are popular simply have too-easy standards. But as Christians, we have access to a power beyond our own to change pettiness to love, to be honestly glad for someone whose worth is recognized, to be willing to measure ourselves against the Great Teacher instead of against our colleagues.

Lord, I need your help to keep me from jealousy of my colleagues. Amen.

Find an occasion to give a sincere compliment to a teacher of whom you find it easy to be jealous.

■ UNLIMITED WORTH

Eph. 1:1-14:   "Because of his love, God had
already decided that through Jesus Christ he would
make us his sons [children]" (v. 5).

A troubling memory from my experience as a high
school teacher is of a student whom I thoroughly
disliked. I wish I could say that as time went on
I learned to like him better, but I didn't. It is no
special comfort to remember that my attitude toward
him was shared by school and community. What
he has done since—and he has done all right—has
been done without the help of our encouragement
or liking. My failure to see the worth in him has
been an incentive ever since to look more closely
at any student I do not warm to naturally. The
human being God has destined to be his child has
great worth whether I find him likable or not.

The situation I have just shared will not be strange
to any experienced teacher. What causes our
negative reactions may differ. Does a student's
attempt to undercut our authority damage our egos?
Does his or her resistance threaten my image of
myself as a successful teacher? Whatever the reason,
my dislike needs to lead me to pray that God will
replace my low evaluation with his great sense
of a student's worth. Next, I need to look for some
positive reinforcement of that worth I can provide
today for that student.

God of love, please match my evaluation of a
student's worth with your own. Amen.

**Give the student you have the most trouble liking
some kind of verbal encouragement and a friendly
smile today.**

■ THE TIE THAT BINDS

Eph. 4:1-5: "Do your best to preserve the unity which the Spirit gives by means of the peace that binds you together" (v. 3).

Many of us who are teachers had inspiring and encouraging experiences with ecumenism long before it became a popular word in religious circles. As our colleagues became our friends, we discovered Christian fellowship with people of many denominations. If we did not worship in the same building on Sunday, we shared our faith and our love and our prayers in the daily walk of the school corridors and the faculty lounge. There is often a real ecumenicity in practice among the laity of which some church leaders seem unaware.

Paul suggests to his readers in our text that it is part of their responsibility as Christians to look at their unity with other believers as a treasure to be preserved. The peace which the Spirit gives to us as individuals extends in daily life to become the peace we share with others in Christian fellowship. It is not a fellowship tied to names like Lutheran, Catholic, Episcopalian, or Baptist. The name that gives it meaning is Christian, and in that name we find a oneness that binds us together, that adds joy and support to our daily activities.

 Lord, thank you for the Christians with whom I fellowship whose denominational label is different from mine. Amen.

Find an occasion today to express your appreciation to someone who provides Christian fellowship for you.

■ THE SICKNESS OF ANGER

Eph. 4:17-32: "If you become angry, do not let your anger lead you into sin, and do not stay angry all day" (v. 26).

In his excellent devotional books, E. Stanley Jones frequently returns to the idea of the physical and emotional effects of anger and hatred. He believes we are so created that those negative emotions affect us physically, giving us illnesses that are outgrowths of attitudes that violate the moral order of the universe. Whether we accept that idea or not, we are unusual teachers if we do not find ourselves at some times yielding to anger and irritation with others and feeling the emotional drain and the physical exhaustion that come in the wake of these emotions. Often our joy and peace of mind flee from us as well.

Not all anger is sinful. There is an opposition to wrong and cruelty and whatever is destructive that may be a healthy response. The Phillips translation of our text distinguishes between that and the anger which is to be avoided. "If you are angry, be sure that it is not out of wounded pride or bad temper. Never go to bed angry . . ." (v. 26 Phillips). Neither body nor mind can rest well with anger draining its well-being. Instead, "be as ready to forgive others as God for Christ's sake has forgiven you" (v. 32 Phillips).

 Lord, teach me to so handle the situations of my life that I can avoid wasting my strength on emotions which drain and unnerve me. Amen.

There is a significant difference between anger and firmness. Take time to think through what it is.

■ WATCH YOUR TONGUE

Eph. 5:1-20: "Nor is it fitting for you to use
language which is obscene, profane, or vulgar.
Rather you should give thanks to God" (v. 4).

One wonders how this verse would serve as a wall
plaque for a faculty lounge, a cafeteria, a locker
room, a school bus. The language of the bar and
the barracks often follows children to school.

The Bible speaks often about our speech—
properly so, since it is often by our speech that
we sin. Profanity and vulgarity should not be
difficult for Christians to leave alone. "Hallowed
be thy name" should be admonition enough to keep
oaths and blasphemy from our speech, although
they sometimes tend to filter into our usage with no
desire or intent on our part.

Keeping our own language clean should not,
however, be all that difficult, unless our aim is
acceptance into the company of those whose
language is foul. Even then, a harder problem is
to know what our responsibility is to them. How
can we provide "clean air" for our students? Since
moralizing only antagonizes, perhaps we can
convince users of gutter language that words which
are trite, unimaginative, and repetitious (all of which
profanity is) are not a sign of a quick and active
mind. We can strive to be the kind of people
around whom profane language seems out of place
and around whom thanksgiving is appropriate.

Lord, "open my lips, and my mouth will declare
your praise (Ps. 51:15 NIV)." Amen.

**Watch for opportunities to introduce students to
words that are colorful and vivid without being
offensive.**

■ SANCTIFIED COMMON SENSE

Phil. 2:1-13: "God is always at work in you to make you willing and able to obey his own purpose" (v. 13).

Most of us are fairly conscientious when tending to our own affairs. We may find it more difficult to be equally ready to look to the interests of others. "I have done my share—far more than he has." "She never volunteers to do a tap. Why should I do something that is her responsibility?" "I could read a good book tonight if I didn't have to finish his report." Yet as Jesus "gave up all he had, and took the nature of a servant," so are we called to minister to the interests of others.

That does not mean we are to take on such an unrealistic clutter of responsibilities that we can do nothing well. Nor are we to shift our time to tasks only distantly related to the realities of our family life or the status of our health.

Some resist doing anything for the interests of others. Others scatter themselves in so many activities that one sees only their shadows coming and going. If we are to look after the interests of others or our own, we need some sanctified common sense to tell us when enough is enough. Then we can do willingly and well what it makes sense for us to do at all.

 Lord, I can do only so much and still do it well. Give me the common sense I need to know what is mine to do. Amen.

Do a little listing of your present activities and responsibilities. Are you doing your part in school, home, church? Are you trying to do too much?

■ GREAT EXPECTATIONS

Phil. 3:7-16: "The one thing I do, however, is to forget what is behind me and do my best to reach what is ahead" (v. 13).

The results of psychological research into the role played by the expectations others have of us is well known among educators: a teacher's expectations of a student will be a strong force in determining whether the student achieves or not. I do not find that very comforting, because I know there have been times when I have expected little and as a result have gotten little response. Some of my happiest memories are of times when my expectations brought about higher achievement from a student someone else had passed up as hopeless.

God has great expectations for you and me. He has offered a prize if we respond, if we run straight toward the goal, if we answer the upward call. He expects that we will be able to win the prize, to achieve the goal, because he made the power available to us in prayer and promises.

One thing that can hinder our achieving the goal is our getting mired in past mistakes and failures. As teachers, we need to take great care not to let students get mired down in past failures. They, like you and me, must be helped to put the past in proper perspective and to reach forward to what is ahead.

 Lord, please keep my expectations of my students from being unrealistic, but help me to encourage them to achieve by expecting all they are capable of doing. Amen.

Before the day is out, write down a list of three expectations God has of you toward which you are consciously striving.

■ TO BE CONTENT

Phil. 4:10-20: ". . . for I have learned to be satisfied with what I have" (v. 11).

Many of us as teachers have probably had the experience of learning of a former student whose beginning salary upon graduation from college is substantially higher than ours after many years of teaching. That experience likely accounts for many who leave teaching for the business world. For others it may take some of the spark out of a day; many teachers might wonder how they can hope to "get ahead" or even break even financially.

Contentment is not always easy to feel in such a situation. It may help to remind myself that though someone in another vocation makes more money, I am doing work I like, work in which I have to a degree proved myself, and that means much. There are many aspects of teaching I like— predictable hours, enjoyable colleagues, intellectual stimulation. Paul had some of these to aid his contentment, but certainly not all. If he were to look at our days he might find them the basis for more contentment than most of us show. We would likely get far less sympathy from him than we are ready to give ourselves. We work for improved returns, but meanwhile we can learn contentment by enjoying the many satisfying aspects of our work.

 Lord, teach me, in whatsoever state I am, to be content—even while I seek to change what causes discontent. Amen.

Make a list of the five aspects of teaching you find advantageous in comparison to other professions. Rejoice in them today.

■ RESPECT FOR INTELLECT

Col. 2:1-9: "He [Christ] is the key that opens all the hidden treasure of God's wisdom and knowledge" (v. 3).

In our reading for today, Paul has some harsh words for the "worthless deceit of human wisdom." This is not the only text in which he warns against human philosophies which threaten believers' faith. Paul's letters frequently warn against heretical teachers. Like Solomon, he advised believers to "be as careful to follow my teaching as you are to protect your eyes" (Prov. 7:2).

With warnings against the limitations of human wisdom as common in the Bible as they are, it is little wonder that Christianity is accused of being anti-intellectual and narrow-minded. In a society that prides itself on being open-minded and tolerant toward differing ideas, the claim of Christianity to be *the* truth instead of *one kind of* truth is offensive to many, even to some within the church. But the Christian need not be anti-intellectual.

If we believe God is the creator and source of truth, we have every reason to respect and develop our intellects, trusting him to lead us into the truth and keep us faithful to it. Christ is the "key that opens all the hidden treasure of God's wisdom and knowledge" and he dwells within us.

> Lord, help me follow the writer of Proverbs who advises, "Say to wisdom 'You are my sister,' and call insight your intimate friend" (7:4). Amen.

Find a copy of C. S. Lewis' *Mere Christianity* and read (or reread) it as an example of truly Christian intellectualism.

■ REINFORCING FAITH

Col. 2:8-12: "See to it, then, that no one enslaves you by means of the worthless deceit of human wisdom" (v. 8).

Some educators believe that one of the intellectual "events" of young people's lives should be the knocking out from under them of the props of their beliefs so they may be encouraged to rethink and reform those beliefs with the proper intellectual underpinnings. If a youth's beliefs are surface level, and not internalized, we can see the possibility of such shock treatment leading to deeper, more conscious belief. Unfortunately, those subjected to this "destruction of innocence" method often do not stay around the one who has shaken their faith long enough for that person to help them with the rebuilding.

As teachers, we must be aware that our own positions are influential in matters of faith and doubt. If we, as the persons to whom the life of the mind is important, give evidence that we have found Christian faith and belief a viable option for our own lives, we may be means of encouraging our students to see it as such for themselves. There are many attacks on the faith of the young. Someone has said, "People seldom lose their faith by a blowout; it is more often by a slow leak." We can prevent some of that leakage by our examples.

Lord, may my example as a teacher be a reinforcement to the faith and beliefs of my students. Amen.

Read (or reread) C. S. Lewis' *Screwtape Letters*, noting especially its perceptive comments on how faith can be weakened or lost.

■ LIBERATION AVAILABLE

Col. 2:13-19: ". . . he [God] canceled the unfavor-
able record of our debts with its binding rules and
did away with it completely by nailing it to the
cross" (v. 14).

Rules are familiar to teachers. No matter what level
at which we teach, we have expectations of how
our students relate to one another and to us. Some
rules, we generally believe, are necessary to a
workable learning situation. Sometimes our rules
make sense; other times they do not. Necessary rules
are respected and even appreciated. Unneeded and
unfair ones are resented and seldom lead to sound
habits.

Paul is concerned in our text lest believers get themselves so tangled up in rules that their allegiance
to such rules causes them to stop holding on to
Christ. Instead, they spend their energies on man-
made rules and teachings which have no real value
in controlling their motivations—and therefore their
actions.

As teachers, we hope that the day comes when
our students can internalize those controls we
encourage, and act out of willing choice rather than
external rules. God too waits for the time when
legalistic obedience to rules gives way to real
freedom to grow as God wants us to grow.

Lord, thank you for new life in Christ. Help me
to live my life out of a motivation provided by
love rather than by rules. Amen.

**Are there areas in your life in which you have
become dependent on rules rather than remaining
free to choose? Take some moments today for self-
examination.**

■ THE GARMENTS OF GRACE

Col. 3:1-14: "You are the people of God; he loved you and chose you for his own. So then, you must clothe yourselves with compassion, kindness, humility, gentleness, and patience" (v. 12).

First "put off," then "put on." How vital to right human relationships are the items listed in this portrayal of a person ridding himself of what holds him back and dressing himself in what is appropriate for God's chosen! Those things that we must put off not only separate us from God but corrupt human associations as well. That which we need to put on not only fits our new identity as believers but improves our daily walk with others.

Did you notice that what we are to put on equates having the mind of Christ? How would these characteristics relate to our role as teachers? Compassion and kindness: how will they affect our behavior toward a student whose family is being torn apart, yet who must concentrate on studies? Humility and gentleness: how will they influence our response to a student who covers a poor self-image by being constantly antagonistic? Patience: how is it relevant to a skills-impaired student who can't seem to learn? Forgiveness: how about a student whose miniscule but endless disturbances irritate us? Then, "to all these qualities add love, which binds all things together in perfect unity." All this we do by his mind within us.

 Lord, these things I am to put on are scarce in my wardrobe. Please clothe me in your righteousness. Amen.

Print verse 12 on a card and fasten it to your bedroom mirror as a daily reminder.

■ PERSISTENT IN PRAYER

Col. 4:2-6: ". . . pray also for us . . ." (v. 3).

How easy it would be to rewrite this passage as though it were intended for Christian teachers called to devote themselves to prayer. For instance, "Pray for us, too, that God may make us effective in our teaching that we may give our students what they need even when they resist our efforts. Pray that I may communicate clearly, as I need to do," and that we may "be wise in our approach to parents and public, and make the most of opportunities to enlist their support." Let's leave the sixth verse as it is. No one can say anything more pertinent for teachers than that.

Obviously the original is better than my version. It offers many pointers for the day: 1. A devotion to prayer with alertness and gratitude (Are you in the habit of three-second prayers—for others? for guidance? in gratitude?). That makes each day a constant walk with God. 2. A constant bringing of our students to God in prayer. 3. The need for tact and wisdom and alertness to opportunities. 4. A way of speaking that is gracious and lively, with what is said going to the heart of the listener's needs and the speaker's intent. These challenges are more than enough to keep us growing today.

 Lord, please teach me the art of conversation that is "full of grace, seasoned with salt" (v. 6 NIV). Amen.

Set out today to be "persistent in prayer," turning the day's encounters into occasions for brief prayers.

■ GENTLY . . . GENTLY

1 Thess. 2:1-13: "But we were gentle when we were with you, like a mother taking care of her children" (v. 7).

Because we see children and young people in a particular context, most of us at some time have probably wanted to tell a parent quite bluntly what he or she was doing wrong with a child. My memory goes back to a mother who constantly spoke in a derogatory way about her son in his presence. I am sure she loved him dearly, but to judge from what she said, he was only an embarrassment to her. Naturally, he had a real problem with self-confidence.

Our text shows a delightful portrayal of Paul. Fiery and forceful as he could be at times, here he is the picture of gentleness and sensitivity to the believers in his charge, "like a mother taking care of her children." Again, "we treated each one of you just as a father treats his own children. We encouraged you, we comforted you" (vv. 11-12). These young believers, recently out of paganism, must have needed much of that kind of love.

So do our students in our hectic, pressuring society. If we as adults need constant reinforcement, love, and encouragement (and we do), so too do those students with whom we work need that assistance toward self-confidence and inner strength. Gentle firmness with love is a real gift.

 Lord, make me constantly sensitive to the needs of individual students for positive support and encouragement. Amen.

Find some occasion for giving praise to a student who doesn't very often get any.

■ A HOPE SECURED

1 Tim. 4:1-10: "We struggle and work hard, because we have placed our hope in the living God" (v. 10).

What motivates us is of great importance, especially when we must continue to do the same activity over a period of years and still do it well. It helps that each child or young person is unique. Yet, even considering that, what keeps us invigorated is the knowledge that our main motivation is that "we have placed our hope in the living God," and him we would please.

Opponents of teacher tenure often complain that once a teacher has tenure he or she exerts less effort, loses the motivation to improve on the job, and begins to coast along. Perhaps we know of such instances, even if we reject the idea that such slacking off is typical. We all know that the twentieth time we teach a course is less enjoyable than the fifth.

The standards we seek to uphold in our perform-ance as teachers should come from within us rather than have to be imposed from the outside. "We struggle and work hard, because we have placed our hope in the living God" applies to us as well as to Paul and Timothy. Those we seek to teach are precious to the living God. That helps us to see them as worthy of the best we can do.

Lord, may my desire to please you lead to my constant improvement as a teacher. Amen.

Put in writing a list of five ways in which you have improved as a teacher in the past five years.

■ GANGRENOUS TALK

2 Tim. 2:14-26: "Remind your people of this, and give them a solemn warning in God's presence not to fight over words. It does no good, but only ruins the people who listen" (v. 14).

The Lord's servant must not quarrel. He must be kind toward all, a good and patient teacher" (v. 24). Again and again God's Word comes back to our speech and the control we exercise over it. The book of Proverbs and the letters of Paul are especially full of admonitions against the quarrelsome, contentious spirit which expresses itself in constant argumentativeness and sniper attack on others. Since that kind of approach is almost infallibly designed to turn students and colleagues off, one might expect it to be rare among teachers. But it is easy to get involved in the "I-can-top-that-negative-remark" kind of criticism which can escalate real causes for concern beyond anything that facts can support.

Gangrene (v. 17 NIV) is a vivid analogy for the effects of contentious, quarrel-inspiring talk. It spreads its sick influence, its results are deadly, and while it does its evil work it creates an unpleasant stink. The "good and patient teacher" Paul speaks of knows the wisdom of avoiding such disputing about words which "does no good, but only ruins the people who listen." And even more the speaker.

Lord, help me to remember the difference between knowing and working for the right side of an issue and being endlessly contentious about it. Amen.

If you are among those who "fight over words" today, practice a tactful change of subject.

■ TIME TO REST

Heb. 4:9-16: "As it is, however, there still remains for God's people a rest like God's resting on the seventh day" (v. 9).

Readers have likely often responded with puzzlement to the Genesis account of creation that tells us God "rests" on the seventh day. The Good News Bible simply reports "God finished what he was doing and stopped working" (Gen. 2:2). Even God stopped working, but some teachers seem to believe they are never to do that.

We have grown up in a society that sees greater merit in constant activity than in occasional rest. We all know teachers who live lives of frantic activity—teaching, family life, church activity, personal tasks; all are carefully clocked for so many minutes, busily filled up, crossed off the list, and started over. Too often the result is tension and snappishness, both in school and elsewhere.

Jesus invited his disciples, "Let us go off by ourselves to some place where we will be alone and you can rest a while" (Mark 6:31). We too need to hear and heed those words. There must be a time for in-filling if the out-flowing is to be fruitful. As our text says, we have a rest coming like that of God when he stopped working. We need to learn when the appropriate answer to more demands on our time should be "No, I need to go apart and rest a while."

Lord, help me to exercise control over my time and energies. Amen.

Look at your activities for the week and decide where you can schedule a half hour a day for your personal quiet time.

■ INTELLECTUALLY ALIVE

Heb. 5:11—6:3: "Solid food, on the other hand, is for adults, who through practice are able to distinguish between good and evil" (5:14).

My language has to stay on third-grade level," the charming, motherly teacher told me, "and by the end of the year my mind wants to stay there too." In summer school, college-text vocabularies were a challenge for her, but she delighted in dealing with adult literature and issues.

Even for those of us who teach, it is easy to feed our intellectual lives with pablum. "Solid food" takes chewing. Yet how necessary, if we are to make learning an exciting challenge for our students, that we continue to be learners, to be travelers on that vast ocean of knowledge. If we are content to stagnate intellectually, our students may soon sense the results.

The author of Hebrews is referring especially, of course, to our spiritual food. There too we need to move on from milk to meat, from childhood to maturity. That growth too our students will eventually sense in our personalities and characters, in our patience and understanding, in our joy and love. Just as we keep reading and learning in our field of expertise, so we need to keep spending time with the Master Teacher to develop our spiritual lives.

Great Teacher, create in me both intellectual and spiritual hunger that I may stay alive in both mind and spirit. Amen.

Check out a book that will challenge your mind to develop a new area of knowledge and read at least the opening chapter today.

■ OVERCOMING BURNOUT

Heb. 12:1-13: "So then, let us rid ourselves of everything that gets in the way, and of the sin which holds on to us so tightly, and let us run with determination the race that lies before us" (v. 1).

To hear of professionals who, because of intensive demanding work, are emotionally exhausted, or "burned out," is no longer unusual. More and more teachers are among the burned-out ones. If more of us are not, we may suspect it is because of the beneficial effects of the summer vacation many of us have. For most of us, this is no luxury. It is the needed refreshment that sweetens the disposition, gives time for intellectual development, and recharges our enthusiasm for our students. It is also a time for deepening our spiritual lives.

But we also need to learn how to experience that renewal during the workdays themselves, how to "run with determination the race that lies before us" with a constant drawing of strength from the source which is our supply. As we keep our eyes fixed on him, we find weariness replaced by energy, faintheartedness replaced by enthusiasm. That exuberant joy in what we are doing is a result of steadily deepening devotional life, of sharing with Christian friends, of sufficient rest and healthy living. As we pattern ourselves on him, we also learn how to consider others and to consider what we teach in a fresh and enriched way.

Lord, help me, when I need a fresh approach to my work, to consider you. Amen.

Sort out today the aspect of your job that you enjoy most fully and really capitalize on it with an attitude of gratitude.

■ LOVE COMES FIRST

Heb. 13:1-8: "Keep your lives free from the love of money, and be satisfied with what you have" (v. 5).

Having either a union or some professional organization to handle collective bargaining is a fact of life for almost all teachers in our day. These organizations can be our way of expressing our concerns for quality education as well as for pressing for a fair share of financial return. Yet as Christian teachers we face aspects of this type of professional operation which can be troubling to us.

Like most groups in the labor force, we are expected to relate to our administration and the boards that employ us as antagonists, pitted against each other as though only we—or only they—have the good of our students and schools at heart. I can understand the economic history of that, but as a Christian I cannot accept the fact that any individual is automatically my adversary. He or she is a being also loved by God.

Another fact of our professional life is the continued struggle for better pay, more fringe benefits. How do I, as a Christian teacher, relate to what the author of Hebrews says: "Be satisfied with what you have"? Can we afford to stay in teaching in an economy unsettled by inflation?

I do not know the answers to these concerns. I only know that we follow one whose way is love, and our attitudes must be shaped by him.

Lord, how would you behave in these matters? Teach me. Amen.

Plan an informal occasion at which Christian colleagues may talk out these concerns.

■ A DANGEROUS TONGUE

James 3:1-12:   "And the tongue is like a fire. It is a world of wrong, occupying its place in our bodies and spreading evil through our whole being" (v. 6).

James' introduction to Chapter 3 is a rather unsettling way for a teacher to begin a day: "My brothers, not many of you should become teachers." Knowing that it is our speech with which he is concerned is not exactly a comfort: probably no profession makes as much use of speaking as a part of its work as ours does. By our speaking we can do much to reinforce and encourage, to create an atmosphere in which love and learning can thrive. By our speaking we can also do much to destroy and discourage, to create an atmosphere in which resentment and ignorance can thrive.

Plutarch records of one Simonides that "he never repented that he held his tongue, but often that he had spoken." I can empathize with that. All tied up with our self-control, our words can bless or curse, heal or wound, soothe or antagonize, defend or attack. We can reinforce a student's sense of his worth; we can shatter the hard-won beginnings of self-confidence. We need the fire extinguisher of God's love to keep that fiery tongue from escaping our control today.

Lord, I know from experience how easily my tongue becomes a "world of wrong." Please keep it under your control. Amen.

Think back over yesterday's human contacts. Are there instances you regret because you said too much? Spoke too harshly? What can you do about them now?

■ SILENCING IGNORANCE

1 Peter 2:13-25: "For God wants you to silence the ignorant talk of foolish people by the good things you do" (v. 15).

Schools today do not . . ." "Children today are not taught . . ." "Back when I was a child, . . ." Do you recognize these introductions? Schools, being human institutions, are not perfect; that is obvious. But most of us as teachers know that the schools (i.e., those who teach and administrate) are often given the blame for what is caused by other elements in society. Junior says "well-a, yuh see . . . it's like this . . . y'know . . . 'n stuff like that," and of course teachers are blamed for his inability to converse when the truth is that there is hardly ever a real conversation about anything in his home. The school is a hotbed of drug and alcohol and promotion, but Junior had the first real access to them in his home.

What do we as teachers do in the face of uninformed criticism? Certainly not throw off responsibility and claim perfection. Our text has a constructive suggestion: "silence ignorant talk . . . by the good things you do," and "place [your] hopes in God, the righteous Judge." Consistent and conscientious attention to the essentials of our work will be recognized in the long run, and we will not have wasted our energies battling misinformation and faulty judgments.

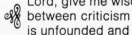 Lord, give me wisdom to tell the difference between criticism that is useful and that which is unfounded and should be disregarded. Amen.

Think out one criticism you know is being made of your school. If you agree with it and can do something about it, decide how to act. If not, forget it.

■ A GREAT SUFFICIENCY

2 Peter 1:1-11: "God's divine power has given us everything we need" (v. 3).

What an almost unbelievable promise—his "divine power has given us everything we need"! We spend a lifetime learning how to receive, how to appropriate for ourselves and our daily lives this great sufficiency. What does such a promise mean for us as teachers?

One thing for which I need to use some of that great sufficiency is in learning to stop worshipping my own daily schedule so I can allow interruptions to my (supposedly) efficient use of my time. I must get such-and-such done in my free hour, but that is just the time a student who needs to talk with someone comes in, and at the end of the hour such-and-such is only half done. What struggles to overcome impatience and resentment! How much I need patience and love! How I need to remember that "God's divine power has given us everything we need." It doesn't happen always yet, but the day is coming when I shall be able to put aside my pen, even in a busy hour, and relax rather than grow tense when an unexpected claim on my time appears. Even when I must say, "I haven't the time right now, but . . . ," I will be able to do it in such a way that love shines through. I believe that because I am confident he isn't finished with me yet; I am still in process.

 Lord, help me to overcome my fondness for my own convenience and to be glad to share myself with others. Amen.

Try today to leave some little gaps in your schedule for the unexpected needs of others.

■ BACK INTO THE DEEP

2 Peter 3:8-15: "The Lord is not slow to do what he has promised, as some think. Instead, he is patient with you, . . ." (v. 9).

A man on a beach who went about throwing stranded starfish as far as he could back into the ocean explained his actions by saying, "There is hope if the outward pull is strong enough." That is the kind of thing God advocates. He never gives up on anyone who may be brought to a realization of his love.

So it should be with us as teachers. Just as God never decides that we are hopeless, that there is no use in spending more of his love and energy on us, so we are never to write off any of those we work with as hopeless. Yet all of us who have been in our profession for any length of time know this temptation. But we know too that the one our feelings would first tell us is hopeless is the one who needs help and forbearance the most. That student is likely the least happy, the least able to change his or her attitude to one we would find more positive. Maybe there are those for whom we can do nothing, but it is not for us to make that decision and cease our efforts. "There is hope if the outward pull is strong enough" to grant them a new opportunity.

Lord, keep me from ever giving up on any student, no matter how he or she taxes my patience. Amen.

Keep thinking today about how to challenge your most difficult student until you have thought of one more device to win a response.

■ PROFESSIONAL COMPLAINERS

Jude, verses 5-25: "These people [whom God will judge] are always grumbling and blaming others" (v. 16).

Developing the habit of grumbling has much in common with the growth of a mold or the spread of cancer. Give host to a little, and it will spread throughout an entire body. Most of us can bring evidence from our own experience of the way in which grumbling and discontent, limited to a few members of a faculty at first, can seem to become contagious and permeate the whole group. One watches with bewilderment, wondering if even Christian teachers realize what is happening to themselves spiritually as they submit to this addictive and constant negativism.

In his *The Great Divorce*, C. S. Lewis' persona speaks of a being who had once been a woman but who now had become only a grumble. Her habit had drained the humanity from her.

To refrain from being a persistent malcontent is not the same as to be an unrealistic Pollyanna. It is not to submit without protest to arbitrary or inept leadership. It is not to be self-righteously smug. It is to refuse to let oneself be ruled by negatives, to refuse to let what we disapprove of turn us into the kind of people we ourselves can't bear, complainers who become a burden for everyone.

 Dear Lord, grant me the gift of contentment, even in the face of that which I seek to change. Amen.

Try at least three times today to deliberately forbid yourself to grumble, to find instead a more useful way to respond to what irks you.

■ OUR BODY LANGUAGE

Rev. 2:1-7: "I know what you have done; I know
how hard you have worked and how patient you
have been" (v. 2).

The other day I sat supposedly listening to a
student's rationale for dropping a class. I sat with
my eyes directed at him, but my mind was still
struggling with an effective way to express an idea
I was writing down. My eyes said, "I am listening,"
but I wasn't. Suddenly I realized he knew I was
not really listening. It was a relief to apologize and
have him begin again with my full attention.

We teachers do not always find it easy to be
patient. We try to plan coherently, then we barely
begin to express our thoughts when we are called
out of them again. What we have just explained—
clearly, we think—is exactly what someone who
hasn't listened calls for us to explain again. We paste
on our understanding smile while our eyes speak our
irritation. When our facial expressions contradict our
words, students will sense our impatience rather than
believe in our patience.

How patient God is with us! How he works to
produce that same elusive fruit of the Spirit in our
hearts. Often it comes only after personal disappointment and suffering. When it does come, we may
receive the crown of life—and be embarrassed no
longer by our blank stares at those who seek our
attention.

Lord, so often my impatience turns someone
else off. Help me to be as patient with others
as you are with me. Amen.

**As you speak with individuals today, work on
consciously giving them your full attention.**

■ WORDS OF ENCOURAGEMENT

Rev. 3:7-22: "I know that you have a little power;
you have followed my teaching and have been
faithful to me" (v. 8).

Each of the seven letters in Revelation 2 and 3 has
the introductory phrase "I know. . . ." The situation
in each church is known to the Lord of the church.
The church at Philadelphia receives precious reassurance that he is aware of its loyalty and faithfulness.
It is not the most powerful, the most dynamic, of
congregations ("I know that you have a *little*
power"), but the believers there can be counted
on, and they are encouraged to hold fast what they
have and receive the "new name" their Lord has for
them.

Some of us as teachers have the same characteristics as the church at Philadelphia—we do not have
the dynamism, the charisma, the flare of some with
whom we teach. Our outgoingness and brilliance do
not bring the instant acclaim some receive. But we
can be counted on to be faithful to do our work
consistently and loyally and well. We are good at
patient endurance. We have our moments of wishing
we had the color and popularity of the more
aggressive of our colleagues, but we don't, and we
concentrate on "keeping my command to endure"
and knowing quiet joy in the expectation that our
faithfulness contains its own reward.

Lord, grant me strength to be faithful unto
death that I may receive the promised crown of
life as your gift. Amen.

**Ponder this matter of faithfulness. In what three
areas of your life do you excel in being faithful?
Rejoice in them.**